NUR 584

Dynamics of Nursing Administration

for use in the
College of Nursing
University of Phoenix

WILEY
CUSTOM SERVICES

TABLE OF CONTENTS

Section One

Leading Across the Network 3

Four Dimensions of Lasting Change 10

Understanding the Patient Care Executive's Changing Role 19

Seizing Opportunities in the New Heath Care Delivery System 29

Applying New Economic Principles and Methods to Nursing Service . . . 33

Section Two

Introduction 47

The Three C's: Consumerism, Cyberhealth, and Co-Opetition 55

Rural Health Systems 75

Section Three

Succeeding in a Market Driven Environment: A Case Study 87

Section Four

From Case Management to Medical Care Management 119

Policy Challenges 137

Section Five

Preparing for the Global Health Transition 149

Section Six

Nursing in the Next Century 161

The Future of Nursing 175

Transforming Nursing Leadership 187

SECTION ONE

Leading Across the Network

Four Dimensions of Lasting Change

*Understanding the Patient Care
Executive's Changing Role*

*Seizing Opportunities in the New Health
Care Delivery System*

*Applying New Economic Principles and
Methods to Nursing Service*

Leading Across the Network

Marshall Goldsmith

*Marshall Goldsmith is a founding director of
Keilty, Goldsmith & Company (KGC) and a
cofounder of the Learning Network, an association
of the world's top leadership development consultants.
His clients have included many of the world's leading
corporations, and the leadership feedback processes
that KGC has helped develop have been used by over
one million people in seventy different organizations.
The coeditor (with Frances Hesselbein and Richard
Beckhard) of* The Community of the Future *(1998),*
The Organization of the Future *(1997), and* The
Leader of the Future *(1996), he serves on advisory
boards for Andersen Consulting's Strategic Change
Institute and the Josephson Institute of Ethics and on
the board of directors of the Drucker Foundation.*

A major trend already shaping health care leadership and likely to accelerate is the trend toward leading *across* a network of partners, as opposed to leading *down* a hierarchical organization of subordinates. Health care leaders of the future need to know why this trend is becoming so pronounced, and (even more important) they need to understand how their capabilities need to change if their organizations are to succeed in tomorrow's networked world.

CHALLENGES OF LEADING ACROSS THE NETWORK

Here are a few key reasons (of the many that could be listed) why networked health care organizations will become more important in the future:

The dramatically increased cost and complexity that suppliers will face in getting products and services to market. Almost all the major organizations involved in the discovery and development of drugs are scrambling to build networks. These networks are being built through mergers, joint ventures, alliances, and even deals with competitors. Major pharmaceutical firms are investing in university relationships and start-up companies at a record pace. All innovation requires a willingness to take risks and to face the possibility of failure. The cost of failure in tomorrow's world may be so great that spreading the risk is becoming an increasingly prudent business strategy.

The issue of cost and complexity does not exist on just the developmental side of business but on the distribution side as well. Global distribution will become increasingly important in tomorrow's health care market. Several leading companies are building partnerships with their former competitors to ensure that their products receive high-quality global distribution without incurring prohibitive costs. As the cost and complexity of getting new products to market increases, the networked organization will begin to become the norm. Companies will be increasingly unwilling to go it alone, and leaders will need the skills to build and manage alliances.

The increased formation of customer alliances at every level of the health care value chain. The ultimate consumers of health care products, the patients, are increasingly organized in large groups. The individual consumer as the sole maker of the health care decision is becoming the rarity as opposed to the rule. Small businesses, historically independent, are now forming cooperatives that can give them the same purchasing power as major organizations (the state of California even organizes small businesses for this purpose). Medical doctors are forming alliances to reduce the cost of doing business and to negotiate (or even compete) with health maintenance organizations (HMOs). Independent pharmacies, which were getting badly beaten on price by major chains, have joined together in purchasing cooperatives. Individual hospitals, which can not afford all the specialized equipment they would like, are forming partnerships with other hospitals to spread the cost of new medical technology. The increased importance of customer alliances will require tomorrow's health care leaders to have very different skills from the leaders of the past. These new leaders will need to form many more partnering relationships with customer groups and to structure much more complex, multiparty customer agreements.

The impact of new information technology. New information technology can connect formerly disparate entities into one network without incurring prohibitive cost. A recent extreme example of the importance of information technology involves a huge health care provider who had a severe information system problem. When the magnitude of the problem came to light, the company's stock dropped by more than 50 percent, the CEO was asked to leave, and the organization was purchased in a turnaround sale by another organization (which believes that it can fix the system). The degree of importance that information technology is coming to have in the health care field could not have even been imagined twenty years ago. In the future the ability to improve networking by using information technology will be a major competitive issue for many health care organizations. Leaders will have to have not only a knowledge of their health care field but the technological savvy to successfully implement new information systems.

The demand for integrated solutions, not stand-alone products. Tomorrow's consumers in a variety of fields will be demanding integrated solutions, not stand-alone products. This trend can be observed in fields as diverse as telecommunications, banking, and travel and leisure. The health care world is definitely no exception. Sophisticated customers are increasingly asking for comprehensive agreements that meet complex needs, not just simple products that fix simple problems. The old days in which the detail man sold a product to an individual physician or pharmacist are quickly being replaced by a future in which a highly trained consultant calls on a team of customer representatives who consider many complex factors in making a purchasing agreement. Integrated solutions frequently involve multiple organizations and may call for a completely different set of networking skills compared to the comparatively simple need to sell a product. The knowledge required for understanding complex customer needs (including financial needs) will be quite different from the knowledge required for understanding how to sell stand-alone products.

The increased pressure on cost and time. The health care industry was able to pass increased costs and inefficiency on to the consumer for years after this was no longer possible in most other industries. Those days are gone and will not return. Tomorrow's health care organizations will either be intensely competitive or will disappear. The stocks of many health care companies in the United States and Europe are selling at record levels. Shareholders have grown accustomed to high returns in general and are now expecting returns commensurate with the very high premiums they have paid for these stocks. Underperforming companies will be bought (with or without the consent of their boards). Reengineering, restructuring, and continuous improvement have become ongoing processes as opposed to one-time events. The flexible networked organization will become a requirement as the time and cost of yesterday's bureaucracy becomes impossible to support. Leaders will need to be able to use flexible networks to get the job done quickly and efficiently. Leaders who can not adapt to these changing requirements will be replaced quickly and efficiently.

The new high-potential employees have very different expectations. The *knowledge workers* in the health care field of tomorrow will have very different expectations of their leaders than the knowledge workers of the past had. In the past even the high-potential employees were willing to pay their corporate dues and play the organizational game. Very few of today's high-potential employees expect (or even want) to work in one large corporation for their entire careers. According to Prof. Reggi Herzlinger in a 1998 conversation at the Harvard Business School, almost half of the students at Harvard Business School today want to be entrepreneurs. The new high-potential employee wants to be given challenge, involvement, and opportunity—not certainty, direction, and security. High-potential employees of the future will have to be treated more like partners than subordinates. The ability to attract and retain these key knowledge workers will become a critical factor in the long-term success of the organization.

KEY CAPABILITIES FOR
HEALTH CARE LEADERS

The successful health care leader of the future may well need to possess a much broader range of capabilities than the leader of the past. These new capabilities will include a greater breadth of knowledge, a greater depth of knowledge, and a significant increase in required interpersonal skills. As has been discussed, leading in a complex networked organization will be significantly more challenging than leading in a simpler, more hierarchical organization.

The health care leader of the future may need these key capabilities:

The skills to form partnerships inside the organization. In a networked global organization, leaders will need the skills to effectively influence people without having direct line authority. Product managers may need to convince country (or regional) managers to commit to a strategic global plan that may benefit the entire corporation but not be in the short-term best interests of the individual country. Decisions about the use of new technology will have to balance the organization's need for consistency with the unit's need for customization. People at all levels of the company may become involved in decisions formerly reserved for executives. Skills at developing win-win relationships across the organization will become more important than ever. Dictating to people what to do and how to do it may not get them committed, but it is simple. Involving people across the organization as partners is a much more complex process and may well require increased cultural sensitivity and a significant upgrade in leadership skills.

The ability to form alliances outside the organization. Even the largest organizations in the health care field realize that they will need to form strategic alliances in order to maintain a competitive advantage in tomorrow's marketplace. Forming a large-scale business alliance requires the ability to conduct an in-depth analysis of both companies' strengths and weaknesses, a relatively deep understanding of finance, and (perhaps most important) the interpersonal skills to

7

negotiate a deal between executives who may have reasonably large egos. Many leaders in the health care field today may not have the business or negotiation skills necessary to build large-scale alliances.

The subtlety and sensitivity to take a new approach to competitors. Aside from a change in skills, future leaders may also need a change in orientation. Historically, the health care executive has focused largely on *winning* for his or her organization. The leader of the future may have to exhibit a great deal more subtlety and long-term sensitivity toward competitors. When today's competitors are tomorrow's business partners or customers, the entire rules of business change. The concept of *destroying* the competition may become dysfunctional. Leaders will need to ensure that their organizations have reputations for fairness and integrity and that competitors will regard them as good potential partners.

The ability to understand customers at every level of the value chain. The health care organization of the future will often have to learn to deal with a number of different customers who may well have competing agendas. Governmental agencies and HMOs may be pushing for decreased costs, physicians may be asking for more autonomy, patients may be pressing for more flexibility, and investors may be demanding a greater return on investment. The effective leader will balance the costs and benefits so that they will be shared by all groups in the network. This will be far from easy. The leader will be required to understand not only the health care issues at every customer level in the value chain but also the business issues. Understanding each network member's financial needs and resources was much less critical in the past than it will be in the future. Many leaders in the past were not trained to deal with the complexity or the pressure that they may face in the future.

The technological savvy needed to produce a competitive advantage. It is unrealistic to expect the leader of the future to be an expert in all the health care and information technology that will affect the organization. The rapid pace of technological change will make that level of technical knowledge almost impossible to achieve. Nevertheless, the leader who does not know how to use e-mail and says, "I don't understand that stuff," when answering technology questions is a thing of the past. Leaders will have to *understand the impact* of technology and *speak the language* of technology. They will have to have the savvy to see how new developments in technology will affect their organizations. This technological savvy will require not only learning new skills but continually upgrading existing skills.

The ability to hire and retain knowledge workers.   As Peter Drucker noted in a Drucker Foundation meeting in 1997, the ability to successfully manage knowledge workers will be a key variable that differentiates the most successful organizations of the future from their competitors. This ability will be especially important in the health care field. As knowledge workers have become more *important* to keep, they have also become much more *difficult* to keep. Health care leaders of the future will have to make hiring, developing, and keeping great people one of their top priorities. Ralph Larsen, the CEO of Johnson & Johnson, for example, told the author in a 1997 meeting that the development of capable leaders (at all levels of the organization) is one of his greatest challenges in achieving the long-term growth that he knows J&J can produce. The skills needed to retain tomorrow's highly mobile knowledge workers will be very different from the skills required to retain yesterday's more stable knowledge worker. Leaders who make this skills transition may produce a huge long-term advantage for their corporations.

—⚹—

Leading the health care organization of the future will be a much more complex and difficult task than leading the health care organization of the past. Tomorrow's leaders will need to learn to thrive in a new networked world. Compared to the more traditional, hierarchical organization of the past, the networked organization will follow different rules and require different capabilities. Leaders of the future will have to develop new capabilities and skills not just once but continually throughout their careers. The pace of change is not going to slow down. Leaders who can not adapt to the new world of health care management will be quickly replaced. Leaders who can adapt to the new networked structure and develop new capabilities will thrive.

Four Dimensions of Lasting Change

Karen Golden-Biddle
R. Mark Biddle

Karen Golden-Biddle is associate professor of organizational analysis at the University of Alberta in Edmonton, Canada. A founding member of the Center for Healthcare Leadership at Emory University School of Medicine, she conducts executive education and development seminars for North American and international managers in for-profit and nonprofit organizations. Her primary area of research and consulting is culture and change management, particularly in health care organizations.

R. Mark Biddle is a consultant with a concentration on private career counseling. He was the founding director of Emory Clergy Care, a program providing health care, career counseling, and crisis intervention. A United Methodist minister and a licensed professional counselor, he has written articles and designed workshops in the areas of leadership development, wellness, and health care.

The recent changes in health care have garnered a great deal of interest and discussion and also consternation. The ways leaders address these changes will shape the concepts and practices health care organizations will ultimately stand for and the organizational structures the health care industry will use to deliver care in the future.

To ensure short-term survival in today's turbulent health care environment, much leadership attention has been directed toward identifying external changes (for example, reimbursement and fee schedules) and then responding by initiating adaptive internal changes (for example, streamlining costs). Thus environmental change has been followed by organizational change. However, leaders will find that initiating change is the easy part of the health care transformation. The hard part is sustaining change.

How can leaders effectively sustain desired change once it is initiated? How can leaders sustain change when the former world of health care, characterized by fee-for-service, no longer exists and the future world is yet to be defined? How can leaders become more active in shaping their organizations' future missions and identities?

In our work with organizations over the past twenty years, we have observed that the more fundamental and far-reaching the implications of change, the harder it is to accomplish and sustain that change. Once the highly touted and visible phase of initiating organizational change is accomplished, it is followed by an often overlooked transitional phase. It is in this latter phase that the work of sustaining change occurs. The key to sustaining change is to navigate effectively through this period. It is in this phase of *liminality* (Turner, 1974), or organizational limbo, that organizational members confront not only confusion and anxiety but also the potential for tremendous creativity and scenario building. And it is this phase that requires energy and devoted effort from all affected by the changes, both inside and outside any single organization.

We have identified four dimensions of sustained change: reformulating organizational identity, establishing partnerships, institutionalizing trust, and developing structural participation. Underlying these dimensions is the recognition that no single organization can sustain desired change in isolation from the larger community.

11

REFORMULATING ORGANIZATIONAL IDENTITY

Fundamental change of the type being experienced in the health care industry does not affect only practices, operating procedures, and other routines. It also affects organizational identity and structure. No change efforts can be sustained unless organizational leaders within and across specific health care organizations understand how an organization's identity is affected by change and are active in reshaping and reformulating that identity.

Organizational identity can be defined as that which is central, enduring, and distinctive about an organization (Albert and Whetten, 1985). An integral part of an organization's culture, or governing belief systems (Golden-Biddle and Rao, 1997), identity is a key source of organizational stability. It provides a sense of continuity in the midst of change. However, in the midst of fundamental change, even identity is affected. Leaders then must ask what aspects of the organization's identity need to change and what ones should remain the same. Here are two examples.

In the past a health care organization's identity and care delivery structure assumed that patients entered the organization when they were ill and sought medical expertise to be cured. However, this prevailing identity has been called into question by such changes as the advent of managed care, a better understanding of systemic causes of illness, and increased patient knowledge about personal illness. Whereas the old identity was based on a hierarchical model of the physician-patient relationship, the emerging identity needs to incorporate a more consensual model for the physician-patient partnership, seeing patients as responsible for their health and actively involved in their treatment. At risk is the belief in the authority of the physician and other health care professionals upon which the old identity of health care organizations has been based. Will health care organizations expand their identities to incorporate a belief in the value of an informed patient? If they do not, their identities will rest on conflicting models and become ambiguous, and the transformation of the health care organization will remain incomplete and ineffective.

The second example concerns the identity of academic medical centers. They were founded to provide specialty medical care based on the most recent research. In practice, this identity translated into the valuation of research over clinical practice. However, with the advent of managed care, the supremacy of research over clinical practice is being seriously challenged. What happens to the belief in the value of research? Can it coexist with an identity built on clinical practice? If these questions are not resolved, the centers' identity will become ambiguous, and lack of a strong identity will lead to the failure of changes in practices and the failure to work effectively with managed care programs.

Sustaining change necessitates, then, that leaders keep a watchful eye on an organization's identity. Deciding which aspects of an organization's identity should endure is often overlooked in the rush to initiate change, yet these aspects will give stability to the organization in an otherwise turbulent context. Likewise, discerning which aspects of the organization's identity should change is equally important; these changes help impel the organization into the future.

ESTABLISHING PARTNERSHIPS

More broadly, reshaping the identity of health care organizations is the responsibility of leaders in the field, both leaders of single organizations and leaders of larger groupings. Health care leaders must engage the broader community in dialogue that goes beyond public relations. They must support partnerships based on listening, understanding, and sharing with organizations, community members, and other stakeholders in the health care system. These partnerships are best characterized as interactive; all stakeholders are represented at the table of decision making. In this grand design of governmental, health, and community voices, often the least prepared for the dialogue and yet the most in need of health care are the members of the community, particularly those on the margins of power and influence.

Dialogue between a health care organization and community members starts with numerous difficulties. These include the bridging the disparity between medical language and public understanding, finding an adequate place to hold the dialogue, and overcoming the community's perception that the health care provider is insensitive to public needs, wants, and even values. However, these problems are not insurmountable. Dialogue (Senge, 1990) offers opportunities to fix broken places, one at a time. Leadership that can enhance such communication, not only in the organization but also in the community, will help legitimize that organization in the community. This task will not be simple but will build a foundation of trust.

13

The health care organization that does not attend to the vision of public health in the community will be viewed as uninterested. Partnerships based on the longings, hopes, and dreams of those served will give organizations more knowledge of community needs and help them adapt to those needs. The ability to adapt based on an awareness of the community needs, and not only on the changing demands of the health care institution, is instrumental in sustaining change. Those organizations capable of such adaptation are those likely to transform themselves successfully for the future.

INSTITUTIONALIZING TRUST

Institutionalizing trust is an integral dimension of sustaining change. Without trust an organization's efforts will be viewed with skepticism at best and as damaging at worst.

Trust at a basic level occurs in health care when individuals in the community believe that the medical profession will not do them harm. For example, such trust should exist between patient and health care provider from the moment the patient calls the physician's office or enters a hospital or clinic in the search for care.

When organizations incorporate such basic trust into health care delivery, they begin to institutionalize that trust. In essence, they build on basic trust by putting it into practice. One might call this *legitimized trust* (Greenleaf, 1977). Organizations that achieve legitimized trust will be perceived in the community as reliable, responsive, and ready to serve. In contrast, organizations that fail to develop it are likely to fail.

Institutionalized trust is particularly important when health care organizations are in the midst of fundamental changes because patients want assurance that the quality and reliability of care will be the same each time a patient seeks care. Indeed one of the major concerns expressed as health care organizations change is whether their increasingly financial focus has damaged the delivery of health care. When they address only the concerns of efficiency and fiscal survival, for example, they are likely to fail in their attempts to sustain change and to survive the fundamental transformation under way in health care. They will neither improve health care nor develop the requisite institutionalized trust.

Establishing and institutionalizing trust is not as elusive as organizational leaders might first imagine. Indeed an argument can be made that a deep and abiding sense of basic trust already exists between the community and the health care organization. In fact, in only a few institutions in our society is basic trust so strong. Nevertheless, in the midst of today's fundamental health care change, breaches in that trust can and do occur. Trust is perhaps the most precious of commodities for health care organizations. Leaders who are intentional about maintaining and increasing trust, especially during fundamental change, will go a long way toward ensuring their organizations' survival and readiness for the future.

DEVELOPING STRUCTURAL PARTICIPATION

Structural participation is perhaps the most elusive of the necessary dimensions for sustaining change. Structural participation is both a pattern of interaction and an ethical posture. It is the health care provider's disposition toward the health care recipient. **Figure 1** illustrates structural participation, showing the possible combinations of the roles of the health care provider as colleague or expert and the roles of health care consumer as active or passive participant.

Traditionally, in the predominant form of structural participation, the physician is seen as the expert and the patient is expected to be passive. However, recent changes are challenging that pattern, and there

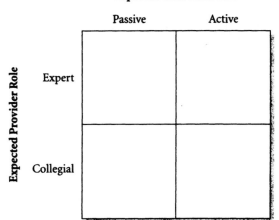

Figure 1   Forms of Structural Participation.

is a shift toward seeing the physician or other provider as a colleague and expecting the patient to be active. For this shift to become fully functional, the health care provider and health care consumer must develop an awareness of their *partnership* for better health. The organization takes on a greater responsibility for communication and education; the consumer takes on greater responsibility for prevention. Patients must be educated about their personal responsibility in reducing health care costs. Preventable accidents, physical fitness, and public health standards are vital concerns. Similarly, health care providers need to acclimate themselves to a more active consumer.

—◆—

In response to the profound changes occurring in health care, organizational leaders have focused on surviving in these turbulent times. This has meant, for example, that they have necessarily focused on adapting to declining health care dollars by streamlining costs and establishing contracts for fixed dollars for services. Surviving by initiating such changes, we have argued, is the easy part; sustaining such changes is the more difficult challenge. Sustaining change requires health care organizations to reformulate their identity, establish partnerships with stakeholders in the broader community, institutionalize trust even as changes occur, and integrate a new form of structural participation for health care providers and recipients. More fundamentally, providers must engage in dialogue with recipients and other community stakeholders about community needs and the future delivery of health care. Multiple organizations and stakeholders need to form partnerships to reconstruct the vision of health care delivery. It is likely that the organization that tries to address needed changes in isolation from the larger community will not survive.

References

Albert, S., and Whetten, D. "Organizational Identity." In L. L. Cummings and B. M. Staw (eds.), Research in Organizational Behavior. Vol. 7. Greenwich, Conn.: JAI Press, 1985.

Golden-Biddle, K., and Rao, H. "Breaches in the Boardroom: Organizational Identity and Conflicts of Commitment in a Nonprofit Organization." *Organization Science*, 1997, *8*(6), 593–611.

Greenleaf, R. *Servant Leadership*. New York: Paulist Press, 1977.

Senge, P. *The Fifth Discipline: The Art and Practice of the Learning Organization.* New York: Doubleday Currency, 1990.

Turner, V. *Dramas, Fields, and Metaphors.* Ithaca, N.Y.: Cornell University Press, 1974.

Understanding the Patient Care Executive's Changing Role and Responsibilities

Diana J. Weaver, DNS, RN, FAAN,
and Joan M. Rimar, MSN, RN

In Victor Hugo's novel *Les Misérables,* the former thief Jean Valjean is confronted with a moral and ethical dilemma. After having been saved by a priest from inevitable arrest and imprisonment and having built a successful life for himself as mayor of a small town, he discovers that his relentless pursuer, Chief Inspector Javêrt, has mistakenly arrested another man for his crime. Valjean's dilemma is clear: He can remain silent and continue to do good work among the villagers who have come to depend on him, or he can come forward to save the innocent man at the cost of depriving the villagers of his leadership. Valjean's dilemma is familiar—whether to act for the good of one or for the good of many. Like Valjean, health care professionals wrestle with this dilemma and frequently understand that serving both goals is rarely possible.

The decision of whether to meet the health care needs of the many versus the one is difficult for clinicians who are comfortable practicing within a needs-driven, rather than a resource-sensitive, framework. And although present-day patient care executives understand the need to embrace the scarce-resource model and its implications for planning and allocating patient care, they also recognize that moving from the mode of *do all you can for all patients* to that of *thoughtfully and critically allocate resources* demands a new way of thinking that may conflict with long-held values.

This chapter presents a brief historical perspective of health care delivery in the United States, and describes the current status of patient care costs. It then discusses the patient care executive's role in helping clinicians work within the resource-sensitive framework.[1]

Historical Perspective of Care Delivery in the United States

Since first opening in the U.S., hospitals have aimed to provide all appropriate care for patients with little regard to either resource consumption or ability

19

to pay. As biotechnological advances and clinical knowledge have expanded, patients have been treated with ever-multiplying goods and services. In the past, patient care took place in large wards where one nurse attended to the simple hygiene, nutrition, and mobility needs of as many as 15 to 20 patients; today, each critically ill patient is cared for around the clock by one and sometimes two registered nurses (RNs) in a private or semiprivate setting.

In the past, little attention was paid to the financial impact of resource consumption or the relationship between resource use and patient outcome or societal impact. Staff nurse concern with the cost of supplies was minimal, and the contribution of the use of available items to patient progress or outcomes was rarely examined critically. Nor did hospital administrators consistently compare patient outcomes on similar units with significantly different expenditures.

Over the years, technological advances and consumer willingness to pay have caused the simple tools of yesterday, such as the stethoscope, the thermometer, and the blood pressure cuff, to be replaced by the complex, highly specialized, and often computerized machines found in hospitals today. However, paradoxically, whereas the introduction of new technology into other businesses reduces the cost of labor, its introduction into health care often increases the cost of patient care. People, frequently RNs, are needed to watch monitors, read gauges, record data, and care for the devices to keep them ticking, timing, and ever engaged.

The rising cost of health care and the impact of that cost on the gross domestic product (GDP) has caused Americans to begin to demand that health care institutions account for the cost of the care they provide. Said differently, resources used must equate positively and significantly to patient outcomes.

Current Cost of Patient Care

Today, health care costs represent approximately 15 percent of the GDP. Economists estimate that if their growth goes unchecked, health care costs will represent almost 16 percent of the GDP by the turn of the century.[2] This would be an unsustainable burden on the U.S. economy.

Many Americans relate the total cost of health care to the dollars spent on hospital care, because hospital care spotlights costs associated with drugs, equipment, physician services, overhead, and daily labor. Although this perception is understandable, it is narrow and incorrect. What is not evident to the public are all the other costs that must be factored into the total cost of care delivery, including associated medical education, pharmaceutical and technological research and development, escalating regulatory mandates, marketing efforts, and the impact of lifestyle and environmental factors on health status.

In the past five to ten years, because of concerns about rising costs, the private-payment sector has shifted its mentality from that of paying for all charges to that of providing fixed dollars for different episodes of treatment. In part, this shift mirrors government's approach to controlling health care costs for the Medicare population that occurred with the introduction of the diagnosis-related group (DRG) system. Another impetus for the change was the business sector's realization that employee health care costs were claiming an ever-increasing percentage of its profits.

Until recently, health care institutions were able to compensate for the lower Medicare reimbursement rate by shifting the cost of the unfinanced care to those patients covered by private-payer sources. This widely acknowledged and accepted pea-and-shell game fundamentally insulated all stakeholders, including patients and health care providers, from the real cost associated with the health care system. However, revenues began to decrease as private payers cut reimbursement rates significantly and as hospitals negotiated further discounts to attract patients. Therefore, cost shifting is no longer possible because hospitals do not have dollars to redirect to cover uninsured or underinsured patients.

Business concepts such as scarce-resource allocation, cost–benefit analysis, and opportunity cost can provide a logical framework in which to address issues associated with the cost of patient care. The concept of scarce-resource allocation compels one to ask, "What is the best use of our resources given limited resource availability, patients' needs and desires, and potential outcomes?" Cost–benefit analysis prompts questions such as, "Do the total benefits (outputs) to the patient, health care organization, or society exceed the total costs (inputs) of the proposed program, procedure, or initiative?" The concept of opportunity cost is elaborated by Russell in the following manner: "The opportunity cost of devoting resources to a particular use is defined as the loss of the benefits the resources could have produced had they been put to their best use—the lost opportunity to invest in that alternative."[3]

However, the business production model of input, throughput, and output (see figure 1-1) can result in a simplistic and incomplete framework for managing clinical resources because of the profusion of factors that affect health and, consequently, health care. The model of a resource information

Figure 1   Business Production Model

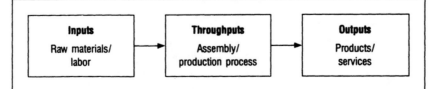

21

management system shown in figure 2 creates a more appropriate framework because it demonstrates the complexity of the clinical, operational, and financial inputs, throughputs, and outputs associated with hospital care.

Many factors affect health care costs, including caregiver education and training; availability and use of technology; and timeliness of interventions. Patient variables in the equation include comorbidities and their effect on response to therapy.

Caregiver Education and Training

The education of caregivers also augurs against managing patient care institutions in a businesslike manner. As stated previously, nurses, physicians, and others have been educated to value the individual and have progressed in their professions with the notion that whatever a patient needs must be made available. To accept any less has been counter to the American ethos that values individualism and heroism. The curricula of health care professionals contain little business or ethics education, and our schools have been slow to instruct students in the solid ethical principles that underlie good business practices.

Moreover, *paternalism* (making people do what is good for them or, conversely, preventing people from doing what is bad for them), particularly in the education of physicians, has created a power differential between system and patient.[4] This power differential is realized when the system does not make complete information on the cost and potential value of planned interventions and resource use available to the patient. Health care professionals must more consistently seek to establish the value that people attach to preventing illness or curing or ameliorating the effects of disease by negotiating the health care services to be rendered given the limited available resources. We must ask what people are willing to pay in terms of both dollars and intangibles such as lifestyle changes and emotional commitment in order to obtain desired outcomes. In fairness to physicians and other caregivers, the research base to support a new model of care delivery that functions within a scarce-resource framework has been lacking and presents a challenge to those seeking to manage health care as a business. This is true for several reasons but predominantly because the complexity and multifactorial nature of care does not lend itself to simple analysis or a linear approach to decision making.

Technology and Timeliness

The questions of which intervention to use and when to use it can significantly affect the cost of health care. For example, the left ventricular assist device (LVAD), a relatively new technology, can prolong life for the seriously ill individual who is awaiting heart transplantation. Application of

Figure 2. Resource Information Management System Model

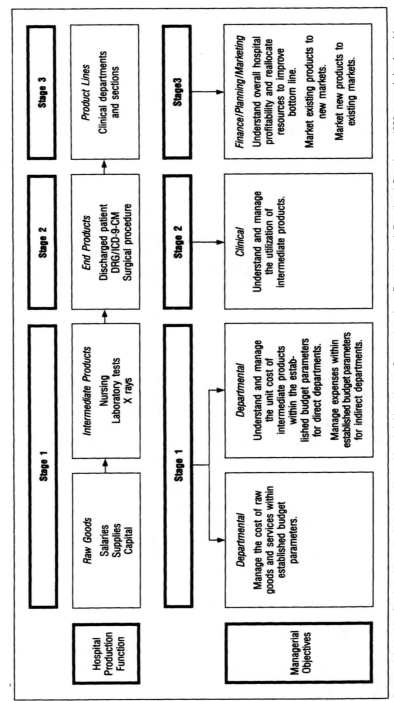

Source: Adapted by Stephen Allegretto, Yale–New Haven Hospital, New Haven, Connecticut, from *Transition I—A Functional Overview,* a 1989 manual developed by Transition Systems, Inc., Boston.

23

this technology is costly, but its potential to improve patients' outcomes has increased demand for the LVAD. The timeliness of LVAD placement affects the cost of care because too-early or too-late placement results in avoidable, noncontributory costs through inefficient use of resources.

The Effective Patient Care Executive Role and Responsibilities

Balancing the cost of care and the availability and consumption of myriad treatment and service options complicates nursing's mission to provide high-quality care to all patients. But with the emerging economic reality that health care resources must be treated as scarce commodities and that, frequently, the health care industry can do more for patients than it can afford to do, the patient care executive's responsibility to provide leadership and management of the core business of health care is remarkably clear. The successful patient care executive will use the fewest resources to ensure that his or her clients remain healthy, well-informed, and productive members of society for as long as possible. Ensuring access to efficient and effective patient care requires embracing a new paradigm and includes the following mandates:

- *Acquiring new tools and skills:* Systems thinking, business planning, acumen for new product development.
- *Assuming new functions:* Managing care across the entire continuum from wellness centers to home care and skilled nursing facilities.
- *Seeking, exploring, and seizing new opportunities:* Perhaps the most important mandate, this includes internalizing the knowledge that health care services will be delivered to patients across the lifespan and creating the appropriate environments and resources to provide desired services.

It also means that patient care executives must guide and support others, particularly clinicians, as they absorb the realities and implications of needing to consider opportunity costs.

To equip staff to manage the situation generated by emerging tension between traditional patient care values and the scarce-resource perspective, the successful patient care executive:

- Uses appropriate cost-accounting and decision support tools
- Educates staff and managers
- Supports clinical inquiry
- Moves toward best practices and standardizes practices whenever possible
- Uses continued improvement and continuous learning as a framework for improving care
- Shapes public and social health care policies

24

The following subsections discuss the patient care executive's responsibility with regard to supporting staff and manager education, clinical inquiry and creative problem solving, and use of research methodologies. The subsections also elaborate on the other elements of the preceding list.

The Responsibility to Educate

Patient care executives must ensure that both staff and managers understand the basic elements of budget development and budget management. In the past, nurse managers were provided little information on budget development yet were responsible for managing huge sums of money associated with labor and nonsalary resources such as equipment and supplies. Staff and managers understood little about the relationship between cost of care and clinical management of patients, including management directed by the strict and labor-intensive clinical standards they had developed themselves. Without a basic knowledge of budget development, it is impossible for caregivers to understand how to implement the least costly initiative chosen from an array of equal-quality patient management options.

It is up to the patient care executive to ensure that managers and staff have the tools needed to make decisions that support the delivery of cost-effective, high-quality care. The combination of today's financial information systems and the expertise of clinicians can produce the budgetary models needed to fill staff and managers' information void and provide a basis for sound decision making. Clinical standards that are supported by scientific evidence (when possible) and endorsed by clinical experts are valuable adjuncts to well-presented budget information in terms of producing desired outcomes. Consistent use of clinical standards and careful monitoring of associated outcomes provide an opportunity for identification and widespread institution of "best practices."

In addition, health care consumers need to understand the relationship between care, cost, and outcome. Current payment mechanisms promote indifference to these critical considerations by insulating consumers from the financial realities of care decisions and interventions. Possibly the greatest challenge to patient care executives in this particular area is to trust that everyone who directly or indirectly makes decisions that affect resource utilization understands the cost associated with redundant or nonvalued activities and acts with this knowledge in mind. A thoughtful analysis of all care-related activities and quality control initiatives is essential to address the cost–benefit issue, and such an initiative is best done by individual care providers, not patient care executives.

Finally, the patient care executive's education-related responsibilities reach far beyond the walls of his or her organization. The patient care executive must ensure the viability of his or her institution by anticipating and planning for change. Equally important, the patient care executive must appropriately and effectively advocate for patients and society in general. To accomplish these requirements, the executive must learn about current trends and act as an advocate and educator through the development of local, regional, and national health care policy.

The Responsibility to Support Clinical Inquiry and Creative Problem Solving

Perhaps one of the greatest contributions that the patient care executive can provide in the work setting is to support clinical inquiry at the provider level, in part to demonstrate the cost and benefit of service. Clinical inquiry begins with challenging care providers to question the value and meaning of current clinical practice within the care paradigm. Suggesting that staff ask why and why not in critically examining their practice is a good way to get the process started. Being able to ask these two questions is tantamount to challenging the status quo—a risky business. Often, giving tacit approval is the necessary first step in the process. For example, following are two studies that are looking at existing practices involving the possible overutilization (why) and underutilization (why not) of skillful nurses.

The first study came about as a result of a detected variability in the use of monitor watchers on units housing cardiac patients. Four patient care units with telemetry capability were using professional nurses as monitor watchers in a variety of patterns. The first unit used nurses as monitor watchers 24 hours a day, seven days a week; the second used them 16 hours a day; the third, 8 hours a day; and the fourth, not at all. Curiously, although the practice differences were known throughout the institution, no one had considered the impact of these practice differences on patient outcomes. Because the differences seemed to indicate the overutilization of skilled nurses, the initial inclination was to withdraw the monitor-watching service on all units. However, the nurse manager on the unit with the 24-hour availability was very concerned that withdrawal of this clinical support would have a negative effect on the patients there. She worked with a clinical nurse specialist and a faculty member from a nearby nursing school to develop a research proposal to study the effects of monitor watching on her patient population, and together they developed a controlled research proposal with funding awarded by an external source. The research is ongoing, and the results may provide needed information on the necessity of a resource-intensive approach to the clinical management of cardiac patients.

The second study seeks to quantify the intuitive knowledge of the triage nurse in predicting the need for hospital admission of patients seen in the emergency department (ED). It compares the physician's decision to admit a given patient with the triage nurse's prediction of that patient's admission. The triage nurse completes a prediction sheet on each patient and indicates whether he or she expects the patient to be admitted or discharged at the end of the ED visit. The confidence with which the nurse makes the prediction is marked on a Likert scale ranging from "not very confident" to "very confident." This type of study may allow for earlier identification of patients who need to be admitted and may demonstrate that the triage nurse currently is underutilized. If the correlation is positive and significant, the admission process can be initiated much sooner, and patients will receive appropriate interventions and be moved out of the busy and congested ED more quickly.

Another way to support clinical inquiry is to provide clinicians with data on resource cost and consumption and to identify patient outliers within a patient group. This often motivates clinicians to question why a segment of the population is different. To use data in this fashion requires that a solid cost-accounting system be in place and that the use of all resources be identified, tracked, and made available to the clinicians closest to the point of service, that is, the patient bedside.

Other supportive measures include ensuring that staff are given resources at the unit level to be able to "scratch a clinical itch." Such resources include relevant journals, in hard copy or on-line; available unit-based clinical experts or advanced practice nurses; and a regularly scheduled forum at the unit level where discussion of practice issues is a consistent agenda item. The catalyst for clinical inquiry might be practice variability across settings without grossly obvious differences in patient outcomes. Similarly, practice differences among primary nurses caring for the same patient population also provides impetus for why and why not questions.

The Responsibility to Support Use of Research Methodologies

To analyze clinical issues in a manner that adds to the knowledge base, staff require support in efforts to use accepted research methodologies. If an institution is unable to maintain a complete research department with full-time staff, clinical staff nevertheless can conduct research under the guidance of only one part-time researcher or with the cooperation of faculty from a nearby institution.

Benchmarking and best practices offer promise as adjuncts to the continuous improvement philosophy embedded in total quality management (TQM) programs. Use of quality improvement tools, coupled with the availability of appropriate data and the mind-set of continuous learning—a concept that the patient care executive must role model and vigorously support—will enhance clinician ability to investigate incremental improvement techniques that are often overlooked. Providing a supportive environment that empowers staff to take risks and ask significant clinical questions about traditional and accepted practices is fundamental to creative problem solving and productive clinical inquiry.

Conclusion

The patient care executive of the future must embrace and integrate the concept of stewardship with the traditional trappings of the role. *Stewardship* in this sense is broader than the traditional dictionary definition, which refers to a steward as one who supervises the provision and distribution of resources. In the greater context, stewardship is value driven and underpins decisions regarding the distribution and use of all resources, which is in line with the current emphasis on the business dimension of health care.

In the new health care culture, effective patient care executives must guide and support others to make the transition to the new environment and to operate effectively within it. This responsibility includes working to educate staff and managers, supporting clinical inquiry and creative problem solving, and supporting the use of research methodologies to add to the staff knowledge base. Thus, one dimension of the patient care executive's new role is to ensure that others are prepared to adjust the business of nursing.

References and Notes

1. The title *patient care executive* signifies the expanding role of the nurse executive. The responsibilities of the patient care executive often include oversight of the various departments that provide direct services to patients, including social work and pharmacy as well as nursing.

2. Burner, S., and Waldo, D. National health expenditure projections, 1994–2005. *Health Care Financing Review* 16(4):221, Summer 1995.

3. Russell, B. Opportunity costs in modern medicine. *Health Affairs* 11:162, Summer 1992.

4. Jameton, A. *Nursing Practice: The Ethical Issues.* Englewood Cliffs, NJ: Prentice-Hall, 1984.

Bibliography

Block, P. *Stewardship.* San Francisco: Barrett-Koehler, 1993.

Jameton, A. *Nursing Practice: The Ethical Issues.* Englewood Cliffs, NJ: Prentice-Hall, 1984.

Seizing Opportunities in the New Health Care Delivery System

Richard Brock, MA, CNAA, RN

Over the years, nursing has demonstrated the ability to adapt to changes in health care practice and delivery, regardless of setting. One needs only to look at some of the recent monumental changes that have occurred in the switch from a system that rewarded manual dexterity in team nursing to one that rewards *cognitive nurses* (nurses who use critical thinking skills to provide new approaches to solving patient care problems) who are good at delivering primary care. Today, nursing is not only faced with cultural and attitudinal change, it is being repackaged to adapt to new care delivery systems such as case management and managed care. Nurses need to view these new systems as opportunities to use their unique knowledge and skills in the development of new approaches to patient care.

This chapter examines some of the shifts in thinking that nurses must make in order to adapt to the notion of health care as a business. It also clarifies some of the skills and behaviors that will facilitate that transition.

The Repackaging of Health Care Services

The notion of "packaging" or "repackaging" health care services is a business technique. That health care is a business as well as a service is evidenced by the naming, pricing, and marketing of specific services and procedures. In addition, the fact that Hospital X offers open-heart surgery and is located two blocks away from a potential patient who requires open-heart surgery is not a guarantee that *that* patient will choose Hospital X for his surgery. Patients are as sophisticated in making health care choices as they are in making choices about purchasing an automobile. They read *Consumer Reports* and select products based on quality, affordability, and a track record of customer satisfaction.

Within health care, decisions as to what to package and how are now made at management roundtables. Thus, the business of nursing has moved to the roundtable, where strategies for surviving and thriving are examined and determined. In reality, nurses may be the only participants at the "table" with clinical knowledge, which gives them a unique and important edge in determining the future of the business. To be successful in today's practice and to be effective roundtable participants, nurses must shift mental gears and develop new competencies.

Shifts in Thinking

In the coming years, nurses must forget some of the old paradigms and shape new ones. (See table 1). Following are four examples of shifts in thinking that need to be in the nurse's survival kit. In the new forms of health care delivery, the successful nurse will need to:

1. Deliver care at the lowest reasonable price.
2. Provide the best experience for the patient and his or her family. Providing the best experience encompasses the processes of admission, treatment, and discharge from the hospital and includes posthospitalization follow-up. Customer service, marketing, and organizational survival are all directly related to providing the best experience.
3. Offer and develop a track record of excellent patient outcomes.
4. Focus on customer services with the same intensity and purpose that any successful business uses.

Competition is part of the new business culture in health care institutions. The hospital that succeeds is the one that can deliver what the customer needs and demands. Thus, as in any business, it is the customer who

Table 1. Old versus New Nursing Paradigms

Old Paradigm	New Paradigm
Success is based on high hospital census.	Payer mix is more important than patient census.
Nurses are rewarded for working double shifts.	Nurses are rewarded for cognitive and critical thinking skills to achieve outcomes.
FTEs are controlled to meet financial goals.	Cost per unit of service is controlled to meet goals.
Focus is on sick care and treatment.	Focus is on customer service.
Focus is on hospital care.	Focus is on caring for the patient in the right setting at the right time.

defines quality. In today's health care environment, quality as defined by the customer is a marketing tool and has business implications at every level of the organization. If health care organization CEOs and nursing administrators could view the business of the organization through the eyes of the customer, questions involving decisions related to hospital decor, signage, noise control, food, and general environmental ambience would be answered. Viewing the organization from the patient's point of view has implications for everyone in the organization, from admitting clerks to people in the business office, environmental services, and security to the bedside nurse.

The effective nurse executive will understand the business environment and what needs to be done from a clinical–economic–administrative–customer perspective. In this regard, he or she is a member of the management team and works with others in the institution's effort to achieve cost and quality outcomes. Because the relationship between nursing and the other disciplines on the management team (for example, physicians, financial officers, and administrators) is vital to the success, and indeed the survival, of the institution's care delivery system, relationship building is key among the new skills that nurses must acquire.

Shifts in Skills and Personal Approaches

Personal development is necessary to enhance any individual's talents. This is certainly true in the health care industry, where the ability to exert a positive influence is key to personal success. It is important to realize that the current crisis in health care is a result of how we are presently thinking. Thus, personal approaches and skills must be shifted just as the paradigms mentioned earlier must be. Important new skills and cues for key behaviors include:

- *Repositioning skills:* The nursing unit is being replaced by the patient care unit; respond to that fact enthusiastically. Invite communication from and with other health care disciplines that affect patient care delivery.

  In addition to clinical knowledge, be able to articulate an understanding of finance, human resource utilization, politics, and customer service. For example, demonstrate that services provided on the patient care unit are associated with the costs of the care encounter, staffing, interpersonal relationships, and service effectiveness.
- *Networking skills:* Do not try to reinvent the wheel; begin professional benchmarking with colleagues to learn about new practices and what works for them. For example, ask a social worker about child-care options for a patient who will be immobile after discharge from the hospital, or query an occupational therapist about interventions and devices that could help a stroke victim regain manual dexterity while in the hospital. In turn, share your innovations and successes.

31

- *Critical thinking skills:* Challenge systems and practices that have become nonproductive. It is important to revisit everything you think and do. If a particular long-standing practice does not add value, modify or even remove it. When viewed as a business, health care cannot afford to retain past practices that no longer work but are kept simply because they are familiar. For example, eliminating the unnecessary moving of patients from unit to unit keeps patients in familiar surroundings, prevents the loss of get-well cards, and avoids administrative confusion in the computer system. Additionally, reward staff for critical thinking and the ability to view changes as possibilities rather than roadblocks.
- *Risk-taking skills:* Examine the risks of risk taking. What is the worst that could happen if you dare act on a gut feeling or a new idea? Let comfort serve as a danger signal. In the learning curve, compile a "what I am going to do today" list and a "what I am not going to do today" list. For example, one might consider the risk of moving admissions to the patient care unit.
- *Skills for anticipating customer service needs:* Go shopping at businesses within the community that are known for high-quality customer service. Once you have experienced what customer service is all about from the customer's point of view, look at your hospital or health system as though you had never seen it before. What would make sense for the customer? What would the customer really value? For example, some customer service–oriented department stores' representatives actually shop for you based on a list you bring to them, and then they gift-wrap your purchases. Consider how such treatment might correspond to patient care; perhaps health care organizations should bring services to patients instead of transporting patients to services.

The reason for developing all of these appropriate behaviors is to influence the quality of patient care in its new forms.

Conclusion

Health care has a new form. In addition to providing opportunities for new experiences, the new form of health care is making challenging demands on nursing. As hospitals, physicians, trustees, and payer groups refocus to form alliances and networks to capture and maximize market share, they have only to ask customers what they want, what quality means to them, and how much they are willing to pay for it. Generally, the consumers of health care prefer to be treated in familiar surroundings such as the home, which has vast implications for the hospital as it is currently known. Nurse managers must be innovative, keeping options and opportunities for care beyond the hospital walls both in sight and in reach for customers. In the new form of health care, the savvy nurse must be thoughtful, innovative, willing to learn, and open to communication.

Applying New Economic Principles and Methods to Nursing Service Administration

Marjorie Beyers, PhD, RN, FAAN

Changes of the magnitude that health care is currently experiencing are challenging nursing's basic philosophy and values. In order to be effective in the health care delivery systems of the future, nurse executives must accept the inevitability of change and understand the impact change will have on their role. They must take time to reflect on ways to direct the changes, learn the projected benefits and cost, and find ways to manage the external forces that add momentum to change.

This chapter offers insights into why the health care delivery system is undergoing change, provides a perspective on the new way of thinking about nurse executive practice, and describes the nurse executive role in developing and implementing the new models of care delivery. It also offers some basic considerations for future nurse executive practice.

The New Health Care Culture

Changes in health care delivery in the United States have been evolving for some time. However, in recent years, they have been brought into focus in large part by the health care reform debate and its surrounding activities. Among other things, the debate has provided the opportunity to review and put into practice the ideas of leading health reform advocates such as Ivan Illich, whose work has influenced the thinking of most graduate students in nursing and health care administration for decades.[1] He has promoted concepts such as wellness and the health maintenance organization (HMO) that now are part of common practice. In fact, the first HMOs were funded as experimental projects and provided the experience for many of the current health care reform proposals.

The experience of insurance companies, based on their unique reliance on actuarial statistics, risk prevention, and utilization control, also has had a major impact on the changes taking place in health care delivery. Although most health care professionals have been sufficiently familiar with these concepts and principles to be able to speak about them fluently, only recently have they experienced opportunities to apply them to practice. In the new health care culture, health care professionals are expected to be not only fluent in innovative rhetoric but also capable of applying it to the implementation of new models of care delivery.

The evolving changes in health care are reflected in the public focus of the day, which currently is on the economic aspects of health care. Cost, financing, accounting, oversight, and risk control are at the top of the issue list. Like other professions, nursing is affected by this economic emphasis.

Today, wellness and health promotion are more visible in the health care equation. For example, the cost of health care incurred by business and industry is reflected in the costs of products and services. However, the emphasis on wellness and health promotion goes beyond business productivity; it also relates to quality of life for both individuals and communities, which is a goal compatible with nursing's strong philosophical base in social accountability. In fact, nursing has worked to improve access to care and the way health care resources are used. These were major themes in the health care reform debate and subsequent actions.

Nursing's Role in Health Care Delivery

Nursing care is essential throughout the fabric of health care delivery. It is offered in every type of delivery setting as well as through independent and group nurse practices. Given the current economic influence on health care, it is difficult to believe that nursing care does not have an economic base or language of cost and price or fee for service. Because nursing is so integral to care delivery in every setting, over time, nursing services have become integrated into the organizational structures of facilities and services. Only recently, the cost of service offered to patients and payers in some hospitals has included a separate accounting for nursing care.

Acceptance of Nursing as a Business

The idea of nursing care as a "business" may seem foreign to many people because they have not conceptualized the practice of nursing as a business. However, nursing's alignment with hospitals and other health care delivery components makes its acceptance as a business inevitable. Nurses in executive practice now have to respond to the demands for managed care, which is associated with stringent resource utilization to meet cost and price projections and to maintain a competitive edge in the health care marketplace.

To most experienced nurse executives, these demands for managed care are a continued challenge to provide high-quality patient care within the context of the current economic environment. What is different in today's context is that the care services are being designed, packaged, and sold to others. Care continues to be individualized but within the limits of a business package, a benefit offering, or a redesigned service with clear parameters, such as a benefit package of a portfolio of services offered at a cost or for a commitment to produce certain services for fixed fees and reduced cost.

Development of New Competencies and a New Nursing Lexicon

To improve their effectiveness in the new health care culture, nurse executives are developing new competencies and a new language to describe nursing services. In order to participate as team members in the evolving health care delivery systems, nurses should be competent in:

- Effecting strategic planning to create new integrated delivery networks
- Designing services in the continuum of care
- Acquiring financial savvy regarding acquisitions, mergers, and affiliations
- Consolidating facilities and resources
- Negotiating with community leaders and other providers
- Designing services that are commensurate with new cost and price structures
- Implementing plans for care delivery within tight performance margins
- Ensuring evaluation for quality and standards-based performance
- Functioning effectively as executive staff or staff and line combinations
- Leading innovations and change
- Helping themselves and others to learn to function more effectively
- Balancing self-determination with team collaboration
- Learning continuously
- Using data and information to evaluate and improve services

The incorporation of business terms into nursing's lexicon is evident in these competencies.

Effective nurse executives of the future see this change as a new gestalt. However, in traditional terms, the change would be seen as a paradox. On the one hand, effective nurse executives are becoming bilingual, thinking and talking about markets and patient populations, developing business plans and proposals for new services, and negotiating for the integration of health care services within and external to any given health care setting. The activities implied in these words are new to the clinical care lexicon. On the other hand, the language of nursing care is being used increasingly by both business and industry executives and the public in discussions about health care. Terms such as *continuity of care, the health care continuum, holistic* or *comprehensive care,* and *care planning* by any name (*critical* or *clinical pathways*) all come from the nursing lexicon. The individualization of patient care is a long-standing nursing goal and outcome, as is the designation of phases of care and the classification of patients by care requirements.[2]

The New Nurse Executive Practice

Armed with new competencies and a new lexicon (learned vicariously or otherwise), nurse executives are increasingly providing clinical input in harmony with long-range and business plans to position their health care delivery entity in the marketplace.[3] They are contributing to the definition of *community care networks* and *integrated health services* to meet people's needs throughout the continuum of life. Consequently, nurse executive practice is expanding in subtle and sometimes not-so-subtle ways. Consider the following current performance expectations related to some of the competencies listed earlier:

- Strategic planning
  - Participate in policy and strategic development, including visioning and projections.
  - Participate in assessing community health care needs.
- Designing services for the continuum of care
  - Analyze epidemiologic and marketing data to develop insights into current and future health care needs.
- Ensuring evaluation for quality and standards-based performance
  - Advocate, measure, and manage quality of care.
  - Identify gaps in care.
- Implementing plans for care delivery within tight performance margins
  - Think creatively about how to design services to maximize resources for patient care, such as designing care sequences from acute to sub-acute care.
  - Execute business planning with reliable cost and time projections.
- Negotiating with community leaders and other providers
  - Build relationships with diverse groups of people in the community.
  - Redesign the care delivery system to improve patient care continuity.
- Effective functioning as executive staff or staff and line combinations
  - Participate in plans for change.
  - Demonstrate and provide leadership for change.
  - Represent the clinical nursing component in decision making.
- Leading innovation and change
  - Improve productivity.
  - Accomplish more with fewer resources.
  - Maintain and improve the quality of services.

Nurses Are Value Based

In the process of developing the already-mentioned competencies, the nurse executive remains grounded in social accountability. It is notable that in these times of change, this strong social accountability gives nurses credibility as patient advocates and guardians of quality. Even as titles change and practice evolves, there is an unwritten but assumed expectation that nurses in major executive and leadership positions will continue to be the clinical conscience for the health care delivery organization. In this regard, the business of nursing care is all about:

- Ensuring access to nursing care
- Providing care for those who require the service
- Ensuring that the public safety and welfare are protected

Outreaching to persons who need health care, devising community and public services to improve health, and working with others to promote the social good are all entwined in nursing's value system and knowledge base.

Nurses think of their business in social terms, and like many others who serve the public in various ways, have not directly related their services to cost and price. However, that trend has begun to change, and even as some nurses are becoming entrepreneurs, their services continue to reflect their belief that nurses provide an essential public service that must be coordinated for the patient/family and community good.[4]

Nurses Are Action Oriented

In addition to being value based, nurses are action oriented. They thrive on accomplishments. This characteristic serves nurse executives well in the business of nursing care because managing toward performance outcomes is second nature to them. The implementation of business plans to ensure outcomes simply gives nurses more tools to use in providing services. The following principles illustrate how effective action integrates business principles into the performance of core nursing care functions:

- Nursing care must be designed and implemented to provide the continuum of care within or across settings.
- Every aspect of nursing and patient care delivery must be managed thoughtfully and carefully to ensure that appropriate resources are used advantageously to serve patients.
- Staffing patterns and plans must be exquisitely planned and implemented to deal with new health care demand models.
- Work flow must be improved continuously to ensure that resources are used most efficiently to achieve outcomes.

- The organizational structure must provide for essential system support functions.
- Effective use of information systems is necessary to enable appropriate decision making at every level.
- Demonstrated competency and monitoring of performance are essential to effective work at every level.

In general, a useful principle in labor-intensive service businesses is that less management is better but sufficient oversight is essential. In any business, key production elements must be identified. In nursing care, a service business, the individuals who provide the care and those who support the care functions are the patient's most important health care resource.

Nursing's New Perspective

The practice of nursing service administration became a formal area of specialization in the late 1940s. The functional nursing care delivery models developed during that era reflected the management theories of the day. A major breakthrough in the unit-based models of care delivery was development of primary nursing care, which brought nursing care to the forefront in hospital settings.

Nursing's new perspective of providing care across a lifetime continuum using all types of traditional and alternative care settings retains and builds on many concepts and principles from the various models developed over the years. Any changes made toward the new perspective should be examined within the framework of three aspects of nursing care delivery:

1. The scope of nursing care
2. The structure of care delivery
3. The science of nursing administration

Although these aspects are interrelated, each has significant dimensions that must be addressed. It is useful to compare each with former and new practices to illustrate these dimensions.

The Scope of Nursing Care

Nurses once provided care in one setting, thereby limiting their service to the patient's requirements within a defined time frame, such as the length of stay (LOS) in a hospital or nursing home. For example, the term *episode of care,* which once defined the period of hospitalization, in recent years has been used to refer to care during an illness or disease process from beginning to resolution. Indeed, for any given episode of care, there might be only minimal hospital use. Today, the term *episode of care* is limited and restrictive because the scope of nursing now encompasses care throughout the life span, from birth to death. And nursing interventions include individualized care as well as group and community care.[5]

Shifts in Demand and Use

For some, the extended scope of nursing care is not new. Historically, nursing care was integral to community and public health and then became strongly associated with hospitals. Today, nursing is becoming more associated with health care than with hospitals. Nursing care in all health care settings continues to focus on caring and health even as care and treatment processes have been changed by technologic advances. Today, there is a very different focus for nursing services. More nurses now are practicing in home care, long-term care, and ambulatory care settings.

The shift of nursing care from hospitals to these settings is reflected in a shift in both the focus of care interventions and in the demand for nursing services. The new focus is evidenced in the adaption of case management, patient teaching, and counseling, as well as physical and emotional care, to integrated care delivery encompassing all care settings. As a result, nurse executives are designing and managing care for the continuum of care, integrating care provided in any one setting into a new gestalt incorporating care, cost, and quality outcomes in every phase of designing, managing, and facilitating the delivery of patient care.

These new models of integrated care delivery are helping to clarify the nurse–patient relationship. Hospitals now are used selectively because advances in technology have enabled the expansion of outpatient services to include major surgery, diagnosis, and treatments and also have reduced the need for some invasive-care procedures. Indeed, some technologic advances promote self-care with appropriate education and support (for example, home infusion therapy). Nursing services in today's health care environment reflect a broadened span of services including wellness and health maintenance, as well as acute, chronic, and long-term care. In addition, there is increasing involvement of patients and families as partners in care.

Other Enablers of Change

The change in health care financing and the drive to reduce costs also have enabled change. Some people choose not to use the hospital more because of increased out-of-pocket costs, that is, higher deductibles or having to pay more because their insurance doesn't cover certain procedures. The new learning on how to reduce costs through judicious diagnosis, treatment, and care alternatives is yet another enabler of change. Decreasing LOS through improved clinical decision making and resource use has resulted in decreased utilization of health care resources. More significant in the long run, however, is the change in incentives toward wellness. Incentives built into financing approaches are a point of discussion. Capitation, vouchers, partnerships, and cooperatives are being discussed with the intent to encourage healthy lifestyles and health practices and improved management of high-risk factors to decrease illness and disease and thus hospital utilization.[6]

The main effect of these changes and others is that the scope of nursing now must be expanded to meet the new demands for care. These new demands can be illustrated as changes in structure.

The Structure of Patient Care Delivery

Integration of the finely segmented components of health care delivery— the hospital, the nursing home, and so on—is causing a change in each. The technical language of vertical and horizontal integration has become almost too orderly to describe what is actually happening in the field. *Vertical integration* refers to integration of different components of health care delivery such as acute, long-term, ambulatory, and home care. *Horizontal integration* refers to integration of like components, such as home care agencies. Initially, integration was considered in facility and financial terms. Thus, the integration of services was preceded by integration through mergers, acquisitions, and affiliations of facilities and financing. Now, integrated services are being formed that allow people to obtain "seamless" health care. The philosophy and concepts of integrated health care are increasingly being defined in practical terms that make sense to clinicians. The focus on integration does not diminish the mission and value of each of health care's components, but it does change the perspective from providing care for an episode of illness to providing care over a lifetime continuum.[7]

The Transition to Broader Nurse Executive Accountability

Formerly, the operation and management of hospital care, home care, or nursing home care were very separate, specialized functions. In the emerging care delivery systems, operational and management functions are being consolidated and simplified to reduce redundancy and improve coordination throughout the continuum of care. These changes are significant for nursing services.

In some settings, the nurse executive is filling a staff role to design the nursing and patient care entities for the entire system. Because the traditional nurse executive role is embedded in policy, strategic planning, and operations in a line-oriented position, the transition to a broader scope of accountability requires a new perception of role and role competencies, as well as a broadened scope of care delivery accountability. With regard to care delivery accountability, nurse executives have been educated to consider each component of care delivery as a separate entity, with varying regulations, payment structures, resources, and utilization. It is clinical services that bring these separate entities together in the effort to design and implement a seamless flow of care. With regard to perception of role and role competencies, traditionally the nurse executive concentrated on a single type of care, such as hospital or home care. In the new perspective, he or she concentrates on the continuum of care for purposes of serving patient care needs over time. Changing from the old to the new perspective is more difficult than it sounds, but the effort proves worthwhile as improved patient outcomes are achieved.[8]

Two Dimensions of Change in Structure

Two major dimensions of change in structure that must be addressed are continuity and collaboration. *Continuity of care* means that the scope of care is extended to match patient requirements for services throughout a disease or illness episode of care, or over the long run for persons with chronic illnesses or deteriorating functional capability (and particularly for wellness and health maintenance throughout the life span). As mentioned earlier, no longer can the nurse executive focus on the time from admission to discharge in designing the care sequences for nursing services; the focus now must be on the entire spectrum of care needs over time and across settings. In this regard, primary nursing care provides the concepts and framework for the new longer-term patient–nurse relationship, which is explained by the term *case management.* Nurses are participating in managing comprehensive care in which the care design inputs of all health care professionals are coordinated.

Collaboration is imperative in the newly forming care delivery structures. It must occur within nursing and across settings where nursing care is provided, between nursing and other disciplines, and between health care entities and the community. The new health care delivery culture focuses on clinical care in which critical thinking, collaborative care teams, and communication between and among disciplines are critical success factors. Finally, collaboration among patients/families and care providers is indicative of the new value for full patient participation in care planning and delivery.

In any given component of health care delivery—hospitals, home care, and long-term care—collaborative practices are being fostered through the redesign of care delivery. Most of the redesign initiatives result in flattened organizational structures and integration of care and supporting functions for care. For example, in the hospital, the coordinating organizational focus for patient care is changing from the patient care unit to use of the care plan, which unifies the patient's experience and promotes the desired outcome. Although both the patient care unit and the patient care plan focus on the patient, their methodology and process are approached differently. For example, in the patient care unit, coordination centers on interdepartmental work. In the patient care plan, the focus is on individualized care. A variety of planning tools such as critical pathways and clinical paths are used to coordinate care in planning that incorporates all inputs in a seamless plan of care. Thus, collaboration results in new relationships and new management initiatives that must be planned and implemented appropriately. Effective collaboration enhances each health care profession's capability to perform.

Although collaboration sounds basic, in reality it is achieved with considerable adjustment in each contributing professional's attitudes, values, and perceptions. It is good to remember that patients/families can tell the difference between an X ray and a laboratory test and between nursing care and physician care. They also know when the different professionals are working together to provide continuity in the care process. The structural changes should facilitate this continuity.[9]

The dimension of collaboration also applies to interactions between and among nurses in the different components of health care delivery. In the past, clients were sent from one type of setting to another (for example, from hospital to home) with a referral, a discharge plan, or an introduction or appointment. Care sequences were repeated in each setting. Now, through integrated care planning in which one person, usually the case manager, oversees the continuum of care, there is less redundancy. In some networks or systems, case managers hand off their accountability from one setting to another. Preferably, the handoff is planned in advance as part of the continuity-of-care plan.

Building collaboration between and among nurses is as challenging as building collaboration between and among persons from different health care disciplines. Effective collaboration focuses on the clinical aspects of care rather than on the organizational practices that have evolved over time. Separation of clinical aspects from the organizational structures and methods is important in redesigning initiatives that promote patient care provided via collaborative practice structures. It also is a first step in rethinking the science of nursing administration.

The Science of Nursing Administration

The overriding challenge in the new perspective of nursing administration is to design patient care service and ensure its effective implementation. In addition, the nurse executive is intimately involved with others in assessing community health care needs and designing services that are competitive in the health care market and that meet targets for productivity and profitability. Consequently, two major dimensions of change in the science of nursing administration are:

1. *Relationships:* The interactions between professionals within the nursing department and the interactions between nursing department professionals and staff from other divisions or departments
2. *Competencies:* The methods of providing nurses with the appropriate education to be able to participate in the designing of patient care in the new perspective

These two dimensions are described in the following subsections.

Compared to the former emphasis on resource allocation and management for specified services in a given setting, this perspective is very different. However, the tools and resources used to manage in either perspective are much the same. For example, in both, nurse executive practice exists to ensure high-quality patient care delivery. Also in both, creating the environment for care and establishing the appropriate culture are critical success factors. Consequently, the expectations for leadership continue to be important.

Relationships

The nurse executive in an integrated care delivery system must integrate the varying operational parameters in each setting around a common theme, for example, service culture. Because health care is labor-intensive, managing human relationships remains central in nurse executive practice. To ensure appropriate resource allocation and productivity for care management in the integrated care delivery system, new opportunities to unify previously diverse staffs across settings, as well as concepts related to managing human relationships, are required.[10]

Some of the most significant challenges for nurse executives now surround the nursing care delivery philosophy and model, as well as the nursing care and practice standards. The changes lie in attitudes and subtle differences rather than in major changes in the nature or focus of the work. For example, both the nursing care philosophy and model are necessary to form the foundation for the operational and management practices in nursing services. Both are basic to designing appropriate policies for the selection and retention of qualified staff; staff development, including in-services and continuing nursing education; and quality management. Nurse managers continue to interact with those from other divisions or departments to accomplish the flow of patient services, but this may take place in care teams related to a patient care service rather than to a particular department.

Competencies

The way care is designed and implemented leads to changes in staff education. In the past, the nurse executive designed care sequences with corresponding tasks, and staff were educated or trained to perform the tasks as designed. Now, he or she empowers others to make decisions and to engage in critical thinking. Shared governance models, often in the form of committee structures and memberships, have been introduced to help nurses make the transition from the old perspective to the new. These models usually emphasize care and quality standards and the application of research to practice. Inclusion of staff nurses, clinical specialists, and managers on these important committees is an indication of the readiness to move toward collaborative practice models.

Shared governance also is associated with new expectations of managers throughout the health care delivery system. For example, managers are expected to use business methods in their work. The increased educational preparation of nurses, the increased ratio of registered nurses to total nursing staff, and more sophisticated information technology are among the factors that have prompted this change to occur in nursing service organizations.

Care processes are increasingly being designed for purposes of costing, pricing, marketing, and managing. Nurses are more comfortable dealing with the challenges of individualizing care than with those of "packaging" care processes, with cost and price attached in a business plan. Care services may be designed in several different ways. One method of organizing and sequencing care to enable assignment of cost and price is the critical pathway.[11] Another approach is to unify components of services by designing a sequence of services from beginning to end (sometimes known as a *service line*), with use of different inputs (such as obstetrics care) using ambulatory, home, and hospital care in sequence. Yet another service design method is to separate services. Designation of subacute care is an example of separating one phase of care from others, giving it a name and a focus. Whatever the approach, the process of developing business plans with purpose, objectives, financial data, and projections of use and marketability are competencies that nurse managers now need.

Recommendations for the Future

The business of nursing care has greatly influenced the emerging health care culture. To function effectively in the new culture, the nurse executive must integrate mission, knowledge, and economic elements with the philosophy and conceptual basis for nurse executive practice. In the transition to the future, nurse executives should consider these realities:

- The core business of nursing is caring and providing support, information, education, counseling, and interventions as required.
- Access to nursing care will occur increasingly through business transactions. The methods of making services available and delivering them will be enhanced by computer technology.

- Communication and information can be transmitted electronically in ways that empower people to act quickly and appropriately. New management techniques are imperative. The trend is toward thoughtful hands-on care facilitated by more up-front design, with techniques for measuring the performance and evaluating the usefulness of almost every care process. Nurse executives are moving to staff roles in which policy, design, and forecasting competencies are critical.
- Nurses must consider their services from an economic perspective. Keeping track of the time of an encounter, pricing a sequence of services, and considering the cognitive power of nursing knowledge as a commodity are only a few of the adjustments in thinking that nurses must make.
- Business is partially data driven but also requires leaders who follow their instincts. In nursing, effective nurse executives will continue to follow their instincts and will keep them honed by keeping up-to-date on changes in business, industry, and health care technology and in social needs.
- The most important asset a leader brings to an organization is expertise and the self-confidence to use it to relate effectively and to contribute. A plan for personal growth and for learning to manage both the change and the business is key to success.

Conclusion

The vision and direction of the current changes in the science of nursing administration have been evolving for years and have recently taken shape thanks in large part to the health care reform debate. The external forces calling for reform have created an environment in which intelligent persons have seized the opportunity to act and are participating in shaping a new health care culture.

In the new culture, health care delivery models such as integrated health care systems are attempting to respond to current economic influences demanding a reduction in the cost of care without a reduction in the quality of care. These new models in turn are requiring changes in nursing's role in the delivery process. For example, more nurses are broadening the base of their practice. In addition to providing services in hospitals, nurses now are extending the scope of their service to alternative settings such as the home. The demand for their service and use is changing from care delivered during a single episode of illness to collaborative care provided throughout the life span. As a result, nurses' relationships with each other and with other health care professionals, as well as with patients and their families, are being clarified and, in some cases, redefined.

In order to make the transition to the new perspective, effective nurse executives must acquire a new lexicon and new competencies and then pass them on to nursing staff. The new lexicon and competencies incorporate the language and tools of a business approach into care delivery. And finally, nurse executives will make the change in ways that enhance the social accountability inherent in nursing's philosophy and mission.

References

1. Illich, I. *Medical Nemesis: The Expropriation of Health.* New York City: Pantheon, 1976.

2. Hammer, M., and Champy, J. *Reengineering the Corporation: A Manifesto for Business Revolution.* New York City: HarperCollins, 1993.

3. Kushel, G. *Reaching the Peak Performance Zone: How to Motivate Yourself and Others to Excel.* New York City: AMACOM, 1994.

4. Weisman, C., and others. Management education for nurses: hospital executives' opinions and hiring practices. *The Journal of the Foundation of the American College of Healthcare Executives* 40(2):296–308, Summer 1995.

5. Bless, C., and others. Nurses' role in primary health care. *Nursing and Health Care: Perspectives on Community* 16(2):70, Mar.–Apr. 1995.

6. Jennings, M. C. Developing a super PHO. *Healthcare Financial Management,* Sept. 1995, pp. 24–25.

7. Blancett, S. S., and Flarey, D. L. *Reengineering Nursing and Health Care: The Handbook for Organizational Transformation.* Gaithersburg, MD: Aspen, 1995.

8. Boston, C. Work transformation in healthcare cultural transformation. *The Journal of Nursing Administration* 20(1):19–20, Jan. 1995.

9. Field, M. J., and Lohr, K. N., editors. *Guidelines for Clinical Practice: From Development to Use.* Washington, DC: National Academy Press, 1992.

10. Kaluzny, A. D., and others. Quality improvement: beyond the institution. *The Journal of the Foundation of the American College of Healthcare Executives* 40(1):172–88, Spring 1995.

11. Field and Lohr.

SECTION TWO

Introduction

The Three C's: Consumerism, Cyberhealth, and Co-Opetition

Rural Health Systems

Introduction

James C. Collins

*James C. Collins is founder and executive director
of the Advanced Management Research Laboratory
in Boulder, Colorado. He has coauthored three books
and published over forty articles. His most recent book,
Built to Last (with Jerry Porras, 1994), has generated
over sixty printings worldwide and been translated into
fourteen languages. He has held faculty positions at
the Stanford University Graduate School of Business,
where he received the Distinguished Teaching Award,
and the University of Virginia. He has taught senior
executives and CEO at over one hundred corporations.
He has also worked for such nonprofit health care
organizations as the Johns Hopkins University School
of Medicine, the Healthcare Forum, and the University
Health Consortium.*

$\mathcal{I}$f you are investing your time in reading this book, you already recognize the fact of change within the health care industry. This volume will help you better grasp the depth, extent, and speed of that change, and it will provide tools and alternatives you can apply within your own span of responsibility. Yet even given the magnitude of the changes facing health care, it would be a mistake to embark upon change just because your environment demands that you do so. You must undertake change within a context, change without abandoning what you stand for, change toward exciting aspirations, not merely change in response to external conditions. In this Introduction, I offer four basic precepts that I hope you will keep in mind as you act on the learning gleaned from reading this volume.

1. CLARIFY WHAT SHOULD NEVER CHANGE

The proper response to a changing world for any great institution is *not* first to ask, What should we change? Rather the proper first question is, What do we stand for and why do we exist? The values this question identifies should never change. And *then* we can feel liberated to change everything else. All great organizations have a set of timeless core values that they cherish and hold sacred. They also have an enduring core purpose—a fundamental reason for being beyond just making money—which they relentlessly pursue for decades or centuries, like a guiding star on the horizon. Taken together, the core values and purpose form the bonding glue and guiding philosophy that preserve the essence and spirit of the organization as it changes in adapting to an ever-changing world. Only by managing this dual dynamic of continuity and change—of preserving the core and stimulating progress—can you hope to create enduring prosperity amid the seismic changes discussed in this volume.

You must distinguish with great clarity your core values and core purpose (which should not change) from your practices, strategies, norms, mechanisms, policies, systems, and structures (all of which should be open to change) (see Figure 1). For example, "freedom of inquiry" might be a core value that should never change; academic tenure, in contrast, is a practice, a manifestation of the core value, that should be open to change. "Improving the health of our community" might be a core value; tax status (nonprofit or for-profit) is merely a strategy that should be open to change. "The interest of the patient is the only interest to be considered" might be a core value; inpatient and outpatient services are simply practices. A shift from inpatient to outpatient services, if done properly, can be a change consistent with the core value.

As a health care executive, you face decades of accumulated practices, strategies, and norms. The vast majority are not—and should not be considered—sacred. Yet they can *feel* sacred. And the only way to break beyond them and also preserve the integrity of the institution is to pin down the very few core principles that should never change, leaving everything else open for evolution. There are no universally *right* core values nor one single *correct* core purpose for all health care organizations. Even though your institution's core probably resembles the cores of other health care institutions, careful reflection will likely reveal idiosyncrasies. Even similar institutions in the same industry can have different core values and purpose.

The key is not to look outside to identify the right core for today's world but to reflect *inside* to discover your institution's enduring and authentic core (for this process, see Collins and Porras, 1994, 1996).

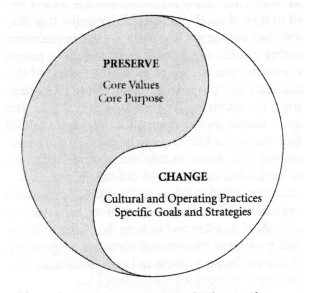

PRESERVE
Core Values
Core Purpose

CHANGE
Cultural and Operating Practices
Specific Goals and Strategies

Figure 1   What to Preserve and What to Change.

Even at this time of great change—indeed, especially at this time—you must clarify what your institution holds to be core, *independent* of the current environment, competitive pressures, or management fads. You must be relentlessly honest as you push to discover what is truly core to your institution—not what you think *ought* to be core, or what industry experts think your core *should* be, or what a ranting management guru proclaims you *must embrace*. Yes, your institution needs new practices and strategies, but you do *not* need to corrupt or abandon its core values.

How do you distinguish between a core value and a practice? You should be able to answer with a resounding yes the following question about a core value: If circumstances changed and *penalized* us for holding this core value, would we still keep it? Only values that pass this test qualify as core values; those that fail it should be relegated to the category of noncore practices open to change.

It is particularly important to clarify the difference between your institution's core purpose (fundamental reason for being) and its business strategies—a common point of confusion in health care institutions. Academic medical centers, for example, frequently speak of their *three missions*—clinical work, research, and teaching. Yet clinical work and research are not intrinsically core values. They are methods, strategies. Indeed, as former Stanford Medical School dean David Korn (1996) has made clear, many academic medical centers have become so wedded to their clinical and research strategies that they have lost sight of why they exist in the first place. A great organization does not exist to pursue specific strategies; it exists to fulfill a purpose, and its strategies must be open to change within the context of that purpose. Your institution's core purpose, as distinct from its strategies, should remain intact for centuries. Yet even though that core purpose does not change, it should inspire change. The very fact that purpose, like that guiding star on the horizon, can be pursued but never fully realized means that you can never stop stimulating change and progress so that the institution can live more fully to the purpose.

I find many so-called mission statements to be a muddled stew of purpose, values, aspirations, goals, practices, behaviors, tactics, and strategies, jumbled together and lacking the clarity to be a useful tool. To successfully preserve the core and stimulate progress, you have got to unravel this confusing mixture and gain ruthless clarity. Only then can you successfully decouple what is truly sacred and should never change from that which should be open to change.

50

2. PROMULGATE THE GENIUS OF *AND*

Health care institutions attract people motivated in their work by deeply held values and a noble cause—people like you. Yet this motivation can block productive change and progress if adapting to increasing competitive market pressures produces fear that "we will become just like any other profit-making business" or that "we will run the risk of losing our sense of social mission." I am struck by how many health care professionals fall prey to the tyranny of *or*—the false belief that they face such choices as gaining efficiency *or* gaining quality, fulfilling a higher purpose *or* making money, preserving core values *or* creating success in a changing market place, and so on.

The trick, of course, is to reject the tyranny of *or* and embrace the genius of *and*. An organization can be efficient *and* deliver exceptional quality, pursue a noble purpose *and* make money, preserve core values *and* create success in a rapidly changing world. Health care institutions have the great advantage of being engaged in work that directly affects the well-being of people. It would be tragic to see these institutions capitulate their core values and noble purpose in the false belief that they must choose their economic viability over their principles. It would be equally tragic if they undermined their ability to thrive and function in the false belief that they must choose core principles over economic strength. No, they must do all these things, and as a health care executive, one of your great tasks is to help those around you to live by *and*, not die by *or*.

3. DECIDE NOT ONLY WHAT TO ADD, BUT ALSO WHAT TO REMOVE

In our hyper-action-oriented Western culture, we respond to challenge and change primarily by adding stuff—new initiatives, new programs, new strategies, new policies, new goals, new imperatives. We add, we clutter, we pile on. And in so doing we neglect the critical question of what to *not* add and what to remove. Let me use a personal example to illustrate. I love to read books and reflect thoughtfully on what I have read. So to stimulate progress in reading and reflection, I set a goal to read and reflect on one hundred books a year. Being a typical American, I launched this effort by adding to an already cluttered life: stacks of new books; long to-read lists; and new reading lamps, desks, chairs, and so on. And yet I continued to fall far short of my reading and reflection goals. Then it dawned on me: the television. Get rid of the television! And so my wife and I unplugged our TV. We no longer have a television set in our home. The silence is blissful, and my reading productivity (not to mention my time to listen to great music) has soared—not quite to one hundred books a year, but about double what it was before.

As a health care executive you probably have a healthy to-do list and a lengthy list of new priorities and initiatives for your organization. But have you paused to ask explicitly, What should we *stop* doing? What should we unplug? Unplugging is one of the most catalytic steps you can take. And it applies across the board, from unplugging business strategies to unplugging policies, procedures, practices, systems, and mechanisms of all types. Health care organizations are in the business of *doing good* for people. Yet this very fact makes it difficult to decide what to not do and what to stop doing. A core value to "be of service" or a purpose "to improve human health in our community" does not mean that an organization should provide *all* services and improve *all* human health. A great organization says no to products and services that simply do not fit, no matter how common at other companies in its industry. In thinking about what strategies to keep, to add, to reject, and remove, you can use a simple three-circle model (Figure 2), adding or keeping those activities that fit in the intersection of all three circles. Great organizations pay equal attention to their core values and core purpose, linking all three circles together into an integrated whole.

4. REJECT SURVIVAL AS YOUR PRIMARY GOAL

At times of great change, challenge, and struggle, organizations of all types can fall prey to a debilitating survival mentality. Health care institutions today face such substantial external changes that some executives, in their more honest reflections, wonder if their institutions can survive in anything resembling their current incarnations. Yet mere survival seldom inspires as a goal. It conveys no sense of forward movement, no feeling of hope for the future, no sense of shaping one's own destiny. The key is to shift the psychology from a survival mentality to a prevail mentality.

Let me use a favorite historical example. In August 1940, Great Britain stood alone. France had fallen to Hitler and his Nazi war

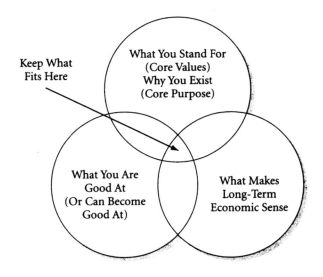

Figure 2   Three-Circle Model.

machine, as had Belgium, Luxembourg, Holland, Denmark, Norway, and most of Eastern Europe. Hitler had not yet turned against Russia and was concentrating on the planned invasion of the British Isles. The United States stood on the sidelines, and would not enter the war until the attack on Pearl Harbor, sixteen months in the future. As British pilots flew to meet swarms of German bombers and fighters, the world watched and wondered—Can Britain survive? Winston Churchill, who at age sixty-five had shouldered the dual responsibilities of Prime Minister and Minister of Defense, rejected the question. The goal is not to survive, he retorted. The goal is to *prevail.*

Churchill's shifting of people's thoughts from surviving to prevailing played a huge role at a pivotal point of the war, giving the world hope and Hitler pause. It is one of the great lessons of leadership from history. Another part of the lesson is that Churchill adopted and adhered to a straightforward yet inspiring definition of *prevail.* For him it meant, "cleansing Europe from the Nazi pestilence and saving the world from the new Dark Ages." As a health care executive, you have to define what prevail means for your institution. You have to *create* a goal. By setting forth an audacious ten-to thirty-year Big Hairy Audacious Goal (not merely a five-year strategic objective) that is rooted in your institution's core values and purpose, you can do much to shift your organization's focus from How do we react to the changes facing us so we can survive? to How do we capitalize on the changes in front of us as opportunities to prevail?

And indeed that gets to the heart of this book. The primary reason to change should not be because the world around you demands it. Yes, your institution faces seismic changes. And yes, an increasingly competitive marketplace mandates significant efficiency improvements, higher-quality care, and lower prices. And certainly, if you do not stimulate progress, your institution will eventually cease to exist. All of this is true but beside the point. The primary reason to stimulate change and progress is the opportunity to create new and better methods of contributing to the health and well-being of those you serve. And *that* is ultimately what this book is about.

The fact that current institutional forms will become extinct (and the institutions that remain blindly wedded to those forms will also become extinct) makes this the most exciting time in decades to play a leadership role in health care. It gives you the opportunity to apply the consummate human skill—creativity combined with foresight—to *invent* new institutional forms at a pivotal point in history. Those who make the biggest impact on health care in the twenty-first century will be those who apply creative imagination not just to crafting new business strategies but to inventing entirely new organizational forms. So, as you harvest the insights of the impressive array of thinkers and experts assembled expressly for this volume, keep in mind that the ultimate solutions will not come from the pages of a book. They will come from people like you—people ferociously committed to preserving the timeless core values and enduring core purpose of their institutions and equally dedicated to demolishing dysfunctional structures and inventing new institutional forms that can flourish in a new era.

References

Collins, J. C., and Porras, J. I. *Built to Last.* New York: Harper Business, 1994.

Collins, J. C., and Porras, J. I. "Building Your Company's Vision." *Harvard Business Review,* Sept.–Oct. 1996, pp. 65–77.

Korn, D. "Reengineering Academic Medical Centers." *Academic Medicine,* 1996, *71*(10), p. 1033.

The Three C's:
Consumerism,
Cyberhealth,
and Co-Opetition

Russell C. Coile Jr.

Russell C. Coile Jr. is managing partner of the Strategic Planning Practice of Chi Systems (based in Dallas), a division of Superior Consultant Company, Inc. He is the author of The Five Stages of Managed Care *(1997) and four other books on the future of the health field, and editor of the monthly newsletter* Russ Coile's Health Trends. *In 1996 and 1997, his annual forecast of the top ten trends in health care was 100 percent accurate.*

Think of it . . . massive movements of Americans of every stripe, embracing fitness, sound diets, stress management, positive thinking, personal responsibility and related constructive practices—a revolution in health status leading to substantial increases in optimal functioning and life satisfaction. And all this during the right-here-on-earth lifetime.

> *Donald B. Ardell, "Health, Wellness and Secular Humanism" (1997, p. 2)*

A new era is emerging in U.S. health care. Beyond the current era of managed care, the concerns of consumers, a spate of governmental regulation, and new attitudes about health improvement are combining to fuel a fundamental rearrangement of the financing and delivery of health care in the United States in the twenty-first century. Seven critical components mark this watershed in the evolution of U.S. medicine:

- Third-party payers are relinquishing their efforts to control health costs, focusing narrowly on marketing and customer service to demonstrate their value as more traditional intermediaries.

- Providers are assuming financial, professional, legal and moral risk for patient care in capitated payment arrangements.

- Consumers with access to extensive on-line information and patient support groups take an active role in their own health improvement.

- Information systems are linking highly decentralized provider networks to integrated care systems by providing real-time information on patient health status, clinical care, and financial costs.

- The health system is refocusing on health promotion for the 85 percent of the population who are the *worried well* and the 15 percent who are at risk or are already chronically ill.

- On-line nurses and home health workers are providing day-to-day management for high-risk patients and the chronically ill.

- Public *report cards* are supplying detailed information on clinical outcomes and patient satisfaction for each health plan and provider network.

This chapter outlines major changes occurring in health care, revealing the opportunities and challenges that face health care organizations and practitioners who must learn to practice co-opetition, use technology wisely and effectively, and meet the needs of people as both patients and consumers.

With managed care in the United States now entering a stage in which 25 to 40 percent of residents are enrolled in health maintenance organizations (HMOs), very large provider organizations are going head-to-head with the biggest health plans in the market (Coile, 1997). HMOs are in retreat, suffering declining public relations as well as profitability. Provider sponsored organizations (PSOs) are tightening their grip on market share, building bigger networks that cover entire market regions. Dominant providers are stretching the definition of cooperation. Connecticut's Hartford Health Care Corporation, for example, is a statewide network of community hospitals, physician organizations, and an academic medical center that is based on partnering, not merger (Droste, 1997b).

Health care providers are retaking control of the health system. The assumption of risk for comprehensive care is transforming providers from fee-for-service vendors into cost-accountable care systems. Employer coalitions could play an important role in the transition. Some employers are banding together in powerful coalitions, like the San Francisco–based Pacific Business Group on Health, in order to demand better deals from HMOs. Other employer groups, like Minnesota's Buyers Health Care Action Group (BHCAG), are making an end run around traditional HMO plans and their capitated gatekeeper models. These groups are working directly with providers in new ways to lower costs and improve care, creating an opening for the provider networks efficient and gutsy enough to step in (Meyer, 1996). Now Medicare is offering provider sponsored organizations the opportunity to participate in managed Medicare, with qualified PSOs federally certified to sign up seniors at the local Medicare capitation rate.

Southern California's PacifiCare has offered to provide administrative services for local provider sponsored organizations that assume Medicare risk. Today's competitors are finding new common ground for business collaboration tomorrow, a revolutionary concept labeled *co-opetition* (Brandenburger and Nalebuff, 1996). When competitors reach a standoff in market advantage, they can switch to cooperation to increase their mutual strengths and benefits. In Houston, Terry Ward, of the Ward Group, is working to develop a local cooperative joint venture involving some of the market's biggest competitors. By refocusing these traditional competitors into a shared business alliance, Ward (1997) hopes they will reduce their development and operating costs and share a better level of profitability than any could have achieved independently. Co-opetition is one of the emerging themes for the decade ahead.

REINVENTING HMOS

The HMO industry is entering a "rocky new phase," according to a recent front-page story in the *New York Times* (Kilborn, 1997, p. A1). The HMO industry is under continuous attack from consumer groups, plaintiffs' attorneys, and the media. Stock prices are slumping, with New York's Oxford Health Plans plunging more than 60 percent in one day, after reports of computer problems and underestimated medical expenses. The spate of criticism comes even though HMOs have signed up more than sixty-six million Americans and are holding national health care inflation under the Consumer Price Index.

Rising *medical loss ratios* signal that HMOs are losing their grip on provider utilization and health care expenditures. The plans continue to hold a dominant position because they have millions of enrollees, but employers are openly questioning whether HMOs should be taking 15 to 20 percent off the top of the premium for administration, marketing, and medical management. A growing number of HMOs are abandoning efforts to compete with providers as *integrated delivery networks*.

Evidence from a number of markets around the nation suggests that HMO initiatives in vertical integration are failing (Kilborn, 1997). In the West, California's Kaiser Permanente is contracting out hospital services to community facilities. In Kansas City, in the country's heartland, the local Blue Cross and Blue Shield organization is closing eleven of its twenty-two clinics, and laying off half of its sixty-five primary care practitioners. Crosstown rival Humana is also dismissing physicians and will slash salaries of cardiovascular surgeons by 40 to 50 percent next year.

Employers are rethinking their reliance on HMOs, and adopting more flexible, provider-friendly arrangements. Electronics giant Motorola launched a nongatekeeper preferred provider organization (PPO) last year, with 100,000 participating physicians and 450 hospitals. In the first open enrollment, 59 percent of employees dumped their HMOs and switched to the company-backed PPO, which is managed by a third-party administrator (TPA), Private Health Care Systems (Meyer, 1996).

Employer discontent is not the end of the line for health maintenance organizations. HMOs can stay in the managed care game by broadening their product lines: for example, by providing TPA services. In Illinois, United Healthcare set up a self-insured point of service plan for the Whitman Corporation in Rolling Meadows. The plan offers an unusually high level of payment (80 percent) for services provided out of network.

MANAGED MEDICARE

The nation's number one health care consumers—Medicare's thirty-five million seniors and disabled—are shifting to managed Medicare. Some 12.6 percent of Medicare beneficiaries have already switched to managed care, the number doubling in the past five years, according to St. Paul, Minnesota–based InterStudy, a managed care think tank and market research organization that tracks the HMO industry (Hamer, 1997a). Enrollment in Medicare HMOs is climbing rapidly, up 27.8 percent in 1997, and could reach 11.6 million enrollees, about one-third of all seniors, by the end of 2001 (see figure 3). Only four states still have no Medicare HMOs: Alaska, Missouri, Tennessee, and South Carolina. That should change swiftly now that the 105th Congress has boosted Medicare HMO reimbursement for many areas.

Seniors accustomed to choice of providers and easy access will demand similar accommodation from Medicare HMOs. Planning consultant Dan Beckham predicts that "the elderly will receive whatever they want. There is no way this group isn't going to vote for their interests when it comes to healthcare. . . . Baby Boomers also have the clout to ensure their parents are treated well by health plans" (Droste, 1997a, p. 2).

HEALTH CARE SPENDING FORECAST: LOW INFLATION

Despite rising HMO premiums the likelihood of double-digit increases in health spending is low. The core rate of health care inflation will remain low to moderate, in the range of a 3 to 4 percent annual increase. The economics of competitive managed care will ensure that health care expenditures do not rise out of control in the near future. Health economist Paul Ginsburg (1997) credits employer willingness

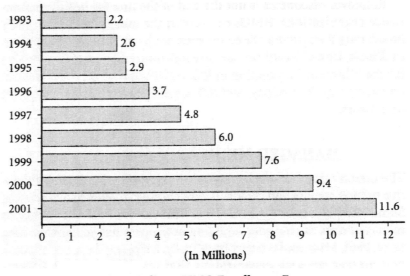

1993	2.2
1994	2.6
1995	2.9
1996	3.7
1997	4.8
1998	6.0
1999	7.6
2000	9.4
2001	11.6

(In Millions)

Figure 3   Medicare HMO Enrollment Forecast.
Source: Hamer, 1997a, p. 6.

to switch health plans to get a competitive price as a major factor ensuring low inflation.

Inflation concerns arise from the current status of the HMO industry. Slumping profits in publicly traded HMOs are worrying Wall Street and HMO executives. The pall on managed care plans is affecting even successful HMOs like California's Wellpoint, despite its recently reported 24 percent net income growth (Freudenheim, 1997). Wellpoint's good news came a day after the Oxford Health Plans share price fell 60 percent. HMOs will attempt to boost prices 4.6 percent, according to the Sherlock Company's annual HMO pricing survey (McGuire, 1997), but they will run into price resistance from major employers, predict industry observers, with actual increases more likely to fall in the range of 2 to 3 percent.

HMOs are caught in the six-year insurance pricing cycle, in which, on average, three years of premium competition and lower prices are followed by three years of rising premiums to improve profits. The current pricing pattern appears to be part of a rising premium cycle. The 651 HMOs in the United States are being squeezed between slowly rising medical expenses and employer resistance to price hikes. According to InterStudy the medical loss ratio for HMOs is now averaging 86 percent, up almost 3 percent in three years (Hamer, 1997a).

HMO profits are slumping. The top 25 percent of HMOs, generally larger, more efficient plans, are still making money, in the range of 1 to 2 percent, but smaller, newer HMOs are experiencing losses ranging from 5 to 9 percent. The arrival of 53 new HMOs, many established by providers, ensures continuing price competition.

MANAGED CARE REFORM

A *patient bill of rights* drafted by a presidential commission on consumer protection and quality is likely to become federal law (Rodrigue, 1997). The proposal guarantees that health plans must pay for prudent emergency care, supply an adequate number of primary care and subspecialty physicians, and eliminate *gag rules* that prevent doctors from discussing treatment options with patients. Managed care industry opposition to this new "ClintonCare" proposal is already forming, and the Health Insurance Association of America has fired back with a threat to "trash" the proposal. Republican lawmakers like Richard Armey (R-TX) have predicted that employers could drop their health coverage rather than comply and have criticized the commission for potentially driving up the costs of health insurance and increasing the number of medically uninsured.

The threat of congressional action comes at a time when HMOs have already signed up sixty-six million Americans, predicted to grow to more than one hundred million enrollees by January 2001, according to InterStudy (Hamer, 1997a) (see Figure 4). HMO's have become the health plan choice of the middle class and of growing numbers of Medicare and Medicaid beneficiaries. The public may fear governmental regulation even more than tight-walleted HMOs and insurers. Although people overwhelmingly favor placing more controls on health plans—84 percent to 16 percent—they are divided on who should exercise these controls. A recent survey by the Henry J. Kaiser Family Foundation found that only one in five Americans favors federal regulation. Twenty percent want states to take a role, and another 33 percent want an independent oversight commission (Rodrigue, 1997). Support for regulation dropped to 52 percent when survey interviews told consumers that regulation could raise health care prices.

Patient concerns about privacy and security are likely to regulate the use of electronic medical records by managed care organizations. The American Psychiatric Association is concerned that "electronic

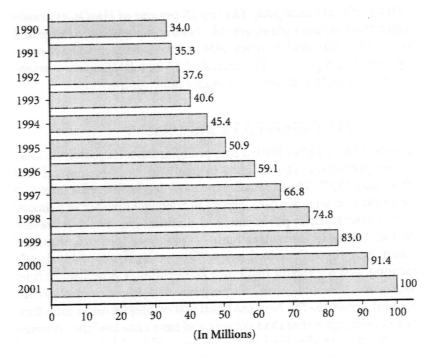

Year	Value
1990	34.0
1991	35.3
1992	37.6
1993	40.6
1994	45.4
1995	50.9
1996	59.1
1997	66.8
1998	74.8
1999	83.0
2000	91.4
2001	100

(In Millions)

Figure 4   HMO Enrollment Forecast, 1997 to 2001.
Source: Hamer, 1997a, p. 2.

peeping Toms" in managed care organizations and government will
have access to patients' confidential records (Wechsler, 1997, p. 16).
The Clinton administration has a medical records privacy proposal,
and twelve health information security measures were introduced in
Congress in 1997. Some federal legislation is likely in 1999, possibly
teamed with antidiscrimination protections. A number of the proposals would require managed care organizations to record information disclosures and make that record available to patients, a costly
process for the plans to administer. The debate is complicated by the
fact that federal action would be an effort to preempt existing state
laws, and argument over it could tie up medical confidentiality issues
in the courts for years to come.

To help reduce the threat of regulation, the managed care industry
is responding actively to consumer concerns. After years of frustra-
tion, health care patients are getting what they want in the managed
care era: access to specialists, fewer gatekeeper requirements and HMO
hassles, and new benefits like alternative medicine and podiatry. Stingy

HMO attitudes and limited provider panels are being replaced by consumer-friendly service and open-access products.

DIRECT CONTRACTING

Provider sponsored organizations have a window of opportunity for direct contracting in Medicare, Medicaid, and self-insured ERISA (Employee Retirement Income Security Act) health plans. Congressional action on PSOs has opened the door for providers to participate directly in managed Medicare, signing up seniors and assuming risk at the local Medicare capitation rate. Midsized and small markets may be the best targets for PSOs. Big HMOs already dominate large markets, increasing their market from 23.2 to 31.2 percent in just the last three years (Hamer, 1997c). HMOs have much lower penetration (20.8 percent) in midsized markets of about 500,000 people. In local markets, PSOs have the advantages of high visibility and market recognition, potentially reducing their selling costs to recruit seniors.

Employer health care coalitions could become "wholesale" customers for direct contracting. Business coalitions unhappy with HMO price increases in 1998 could turn to provider sponsored organizations, just as BHCAG in Minneapolis-St. Paul did in 1997. Stanford economics professor Alain Enthoven (1997), who serves on an advisory board to the California Public Employee Retirement System (CalPERS), the largest managed care buyer in California, has championed a market-based solution he calls *managed competition*. In California, market forces have produced six employer sponsored purchasing groups, including three for small, one for midsized, and two (one public, one private) for large employers.

The trend to direct contracting is still more potential than actual, but signs of employer discontent are widespread. Employer groups in Wisconsin, Iowa, Illinois, and Texas, for example, are rethinking their reliance on HMOs. Corporate health benefits managers are unhappy with HMO premium increases, which are averaging 5 percent in 1998 for large employers and 6 to 12 percent for smaller firms (Kilborn, 1997). In Houston the Health Care Purchasing Organization represents 40 large companies and 2,500 smaller ones and contracts directly with a network of providers. Organization president Ralph Smith argues that "the HMO middleman sets a fixed premium for employers, pushes the risk onto the providers, and then any gain goes to the

HMO while providers and employers take all of the downside risk"
(Meyer, 1996, p. 36).

MARKET CONSOLIDATION

The market consolidation of health plans and providers is leading to
a new phase of market competition, sometimes called sumo wrestling,
in which very large plans bargain hard with provider networks of
dozens of hospitals and thousands of doctors. For plans and providers,
consolidation seeks economies of scale; it can slash overhead and
operating costs and gain market leverage for contracting. Hospitals
and physicians are consolidating at an ever-increasing pace. Regional
markets are shaking down to two to three competing provider sponsored networks, each controlling a share of the market ranging from
25 to 35 (or more) percent. They are facing three to four dominant
health plans that collectively control 70 to 80 percent of HMO local
market share (Hamer, 1997b).

Economics is driving the increased concentration of power in the
hands of a few provider sponsored organizations. In a national survey by TriBrook/AM&G, the top five reasons for consolidation were
reducing operating expenses, attracting more managed care contracts,
improving community health, reducing capital expenditures, and
responding to employer and business coalition pressures (Japsen,
1997). Industry consolidation is rolling up U.S. hospitals, physicians
and health plans into large, regionally integrated systems and networks. Hospital mergers, for example, went up by 44 percent from
1994 to 1995 (Monroe, 1996). In trend-setting Southern California, a
record twenty-nine hospitals completed mergers, acquisitions, or formal affiliations in 1996, a pace twice that of consolidations in 1995. A
survey indicated that another twenty-eight hospitals planned to affil-
iate or merge in 1997 (Wall, 1997). In more than half of these transactions, for-profit hospitals became part of larger chains. Five hospitals
converted from nonprofits to for-profits, and two from for-profits to
nonprofits.

Vertical integration is still a prominent strategy driving health organization merger mania. A recent industry survey showed that hospitals, physicians, and managed care organizations are planning to
acquire each other in record numbers (see Table 1.1). Nearly one-third
of the surveyed hospitals had been part of a consolidation in the past

five years, and one-third of the health plans had acquired another HMO in the same period (Greene, 1997). Half of the surveyed medical groups had been involved in a transaction with a for-profit physician company or nonprofit hospital or health system. Hospitals were still interested in buying medical group practices, despite reports that 80 percent of hospitals were losing money on the physician deals.

MEDICAL MEGA-GROUPS

A new generation of very large physician organizations is rising to take charge of some markets. Compared to their predecessors, these *medical mega-groups* are not only larger but better capitalized and managed and more broadly distributed to provide regional coverage. Many more physician organizations are now taking capitation. A growing number of them are owned or managed by Wall Street–financed physician practice management companies, which provide capital, systems, and management expertise.

Large, market-savvy medical groups have many capabilities that managed care organizations are seeking (Holm and Zuza, 1997):

- A geographical distribution that puts physicians within ten to fifteen minutes of all enrollees

- The ability to manage risk for professional services and, in some plans, global risk for inpatient and outpatient services

- Effective governance and management systems

| | Organizations | | |
Strategy	Hospitals	Managed Care Organizations	Medical Groups
Buy a hospital	47 percent	32 percent	27 percent
Buy a group practice	23	23	63
Ally with a managed care organization	33	42	23

Table 1.1. Who Plans to Do What with Whom?
           Future Partnership Strategies.

Source: Data from Jay Greene, "1997 Leadership Survey," cited in Greene, 1997, p. 8.

- The financial strength to accept capitation and various payment options
- A primary care orientation
- The ability to document quality indicators, including patient satisfaction and clinical outcomes

Physician groups are merging to create market-dominating organizations that swing real clout. In the past three years linkages between physician groups have risen 58 percent (Monroe, 1996). Bigger medical groups have more leverage in managed care contracting, but there are additional reasons for physician consolidation. Sharing the cost of upgrading information systems is a major factor, cited by 61 percent of the groups. Only 4 percent of physicians were submitting claims electronically in 1996, mostly larger groups (Slepin, 1996). Another benefit is the ability to compare practice patterns, lowering costs and improving productivity.

A second generation of independent practice associations (IPAs), medical mega-groups of another kind, is demonstrating that the network model of organization can successfully assume and manage capitation for large enrolled populations (Lowes, 1997). In San Francisco an IPA originally started by the California Pacific Medical Center and later restructured as a physician-owned entity, the Brown & Toland Medical Group, now has 1,250 physicians and 172,000 covered lives under capitation. Brown & Toland recently became the first IPA in California to obtain a state license (known in California as a limited Knox-Keene license) to accept global capitation for both inpatient and outpatient services.

And it's not happening just in California. In Milwaukee the Wisconsin Independent Physicians Group has organized 1,050 physicians to service forty-five thousand Medicaid patients under a global risk contract. The IPA is capitated, but physicians are paid on a fee-for-service basis. The group is using a population health approach to reduce risks and utilization. To control costs, the doctors own a free-standing imaging center and channel all testing through a commercial lab. The IPA describes its physician fee schedule as "generous" and relies on education rather than discipline to manage costs. It also uses peer pressure as another method of controlling utilization. Physician performance data systems regularly profile every doctor's costs, and physicians' names appear on reports so that colleagues can compare performance.

FOR-PROFIT BACKLASH

Wall Street may no longer be welcome on Main Street, at least not in the operation of hospitals and health plans. A growing backlash composed of media criticism, public concern, and state regulation is slowing the growth of for-profit health care companies. Public confidence in for-profit HMOs and health care companies is dropping. A random poll of one thousand Americans by the Henry J. Kaiser Family Foundation showed that the percentage who thought for-profit organizations provided better care fell from 55 percent to 42 percent in 1997 (Walker, 1997).

Columbia/HCA's troubles with the FBI and the Justice Department have been widely chronicled in the *Wall Street Journal* and *New York Times*. Under the twin clouds of massive Medicare fraud investigation and falling profits, the dismemberment of Columbia and the sale of all but its core hospitals is now underway, with two or more new companies likely to result (Sharpe, 1997). Columbia has now announced plans to spin off some 108 hospitals that do not fit Columbia's long-term strategy (Woodyard and Findlay, 1997). Columbia facilities outside the markets in which Columbia now has a critical mass could also be sold. Columbia/HCA suffered another blow when several states joined a shareholders' lawsuit against it. California, New York, Louisiana, and several municipalities have entered the fray, charging that Columbia management had allowed Medicare fraud to "flourish" (White and Lagnado, 1997, p. B5). California's Public Employee Retirement System suffered a $50 million loss when Columbia's shares sank in the wake of the fraud investigations.

Troubles for the for-profit health care industry are far from over. There are echoes of the *Wal-Mart wars* in the rising public antipathy toward for-profit health care companies. Even well-managed companies like Tenet, HealthSouth, and PhyCor may find growing opposition to acquisitions and new development. State attorney generals have discovered the publicity value of opposing for-profit takeovers of nonprofit providers. Several states, including California, Rhode Island, and Nebraska, have recently passed legislation making for-profit conversions subject to state review.

Despite the negative publicity and regulatory hurdles for-profits face, CEOs of nonprofit hospitals expect that for-profit hospital chains will expand their market share to 20 percent by the year 2000, rising to 29 percent within ten years, according to a national survey (Greene, 1997).

CYBERHEALTH

Information technology is the fastest-growing U.S. industry. According to *Cybernation*, a national study by the American Electronics Association and the NASDAQ stock exchange, computing and telecommunications have grown 57 percent since 1990 (Lohr, 1997). The high-tech sector generates 6.4 percent of the U.S. gross domestic product (GDP) and employs 4.2 million workers. *Cyberhealth* information systems today include electronic medical records, enterprisewide information linkages, Internet and intranet connections, data warehouses, distributed PC networks, remote-site telecommunications, and even in-home patient monitoring systems.

Health care information systems are essential to managing costs through disease management programs. In Falls Church, Virginia, the Innova Health System is creating a data repository to track more than 500,000 inpatient and outpatient visits per year (Hornung, 1997). The primary end products will be clinical analysis, quality assurance, and outcome assessment. Financial connectivity is another important goal of automation. Providers are learning to make effective use of their information system investments in such areas as claims processing and electronic data interchange (EDI). Submitting claims electronically can save $2.00 to $4.00 per claim, with some integrated systems experiencing savings of 75 to 90 percent in business office claims costs, which average $7.50 per bill (Slepin, 1996).

Information systems are expensive, and many buyers are still skeptical of the return on investment. The payoff comes from doing things differently, not just faster. Computerized analysis of cost variation can help repay information system investments. In South Bend, Indiana, the Holy Cross Health System saved $4.5 million by reducing variations in the pattern of care for thirty-six case groups (Appleby, 1997). Holy Cross information specialists also predicted the impact of managed care on the system's eleven facilities, finding that the system had to cut $80 million out of operating expenses or suffer major losses. The wake-up call was painful but timely.

Although most health care providers still only dream of a paperless information system, electronic medical records are making headway. A national survey of nearly five hundred physician group practices found that 22 percent of the groups had some or all of their records computerized (Montague and Pitman, 1996). Managed care transactions such as claims processing, eligibility verification, access

68

to health plan enrollment lists, and submission of monthly encounter lists are fast-growing targets for automation. For capitated physicians, automating to reduce the cost of these backroom functions means more net income for themselves.

The application of cybernetics to patient care and also patient satisfaction is widening rapidly. In the area of physician-patient communication, for example, computers can insert instructions in electronic medical records to remind physicians to respond to patient concerns. Doctors at the William N. Wishard Memorial Hospital in Indianapolis respond to cues embedded in the hospital's intranet-enabled clinical information network. The messages are based on patient satisfaction surveys that identified disease-specific communication concerns. For example, doctors treating colonoscopy patients are reminded, "Before you order this colonoscopy, consider that patients often report they were not warned a test might cause pain or discomfort" ("Hospital to Test Use of Computer-Based Reminders," 1997, p. 5).

CONSUMERISM

Consumers have more choices in health care today, and retail marketing strategies are targeting them like Patriot missiles. Media campaigns by hospitals and health plans are reviving market warfare in their appeals to consumers' preferences. In New York, Aetna US Healthcare (1997) purchased a full-page advertisement in the *New York Times*. Showing a photo of a large apple dominating a table of oranges, Aetna boasted that it was the first HMO in New York City to win both full accreditation from the National Committee for Quality Assurance and the Sachs "seal of excellence" awarded for consumer satisfaction.

Retail marketing gives providers opportunities to *grow* their businesses with creative approaches to revenue growth and customer trends. Marketing consultant Ellen Goldman, of GrowthPartners in Reston, Virginia, and Karen Corrigan, of Sentara Health System in Norfolk, recommend three retail marketing strategies (Goldman and Corrigan, 1997):

- *Enhance the customer's experience.* Focus on the "atmospherics" of the point of service, creating an environment in which people want to purchase services. Attend to decor, displays, signage, selling techniques, and customer service. For example, offer waiting rooms that look like hotel lobbies, not airport holding areas. Winners of Modern Healthcare's 1997 design awards for health facilities were praised for their "patient-driven architecture," which featured residential characteristics and a family orientation (Pinto, 1997, p. 47).

• *Meet the customer's related needs.* Take opportunities to present and sell related products or services. Stimulating additional spending responds to customers' needs for convenience. For example, situating a home health agency outlet adjacent to heavy hospital patient and visitor traffic may stimulate additional business.

• *Segment products and markets.* Identify the unmet needs of people by age, sex, ethnicity, income, or other demographically defined subgroup. Marketers look for product or service variations that are tailored to a specific set of customers, for example, small businesses. Market gaps are unrecognized segments or products. In health care services, for example, adolescent medicine is aimed at youths aged fourteen to nineteen who may be too old to be pediatric patients but who do not want to share their parents' practitioners.

COMPLEMENTARY MEDICINE

Alternative medicine has almost reached mainstream acceptance. Its latest name is *complementary medicine,* a new label for treatments once called *unconventional.* Acupuncture, biofeedback, chiropractic, herbal remedies and homeopathy, nutrition, osteopathy, and yoga have arrived to join mainstream medical care. A marketing blitz by health plans and hospitals intends to capture consumers who have been spending $10 billion a year of out-of-pocket cash for health promotion and wellness.

Complementary medicine is popular with managed care enrollees, and a half-dozen national HMOs have begun to offer some complementary medicine benefits. National health plans, for example, have begun running multipage advertisements in newspapers such as the *New York Times* to announce this different philosophy and new attitude toward the delivery of health care services. HMOs are trumpeting newly credentialed networks of alternative medical providers.

In Dallas the "new medicine" was the subject of a widely attended medical conference sponsored by the University of Texas's Southwest Medical School and drawing 1,200 participants (Peterson, 1997).

The payoff in offering complementary medicine may be more than a marketing advantage. HMOs experimenting with alternative therapies are finding real cost benefit. According to Herbert Benson, M.D., head of Boston's Mind/Body Medical Institute, HMOs can experience a 50 percent reduction in stress-related injuries and 30 percent fewer visits for chronic back pain by training patients in self-relaxation and stress management (Montague, 1996).

Finally, the public's current high interest in health and wellness may have profit potential. For example, former Columbia/HCA executive Richard Scott is reentering the health industry from an unexpected direction—consumer health information. Scott and former second-in-command David Vandewater have purchased a majority stake in America's Health Network, a Florida-based cable channel that was the target of a Columbia acquisition offer until Richard Scott's departure as head of Columbia. The network features such programs as "Ask the Doctor" and currently reaches about 6.5 million households (Lagnado, 1997).

References

Aetna US Healthcare. "The More You Compare Health Care Companies, the More You Realize There Is No Comparison." Advertisement. *New York Times,* Nov. 12, 1997, p. A15.

Appleby, C. "Payoff @ InfoTech.Now." *Hospitals & Health Networks,* 1997, *71*(19), 59–60.

Ardell, D. B. *Health, Wellness and Secular Humanism.* Amherst, N.Y.: Council for Secular Humanism, 1997.

Brandenburger, A. M., and Nalebuff, B. J. *Co-Opetition.* New York: Doubleday, 1996.

Coile, R. C., Jr. *The Five Stages of Managed Care.* Chicago: Health Administration Press, 1997.

Droste, T. M. "Health System Marketers Must Learn from Past Mistakes So History Won't Repeat Itself." *Medical Network Strategy Report,* Sept. 1997a, pp. 1–4.

Droste, T. M. "One System Relies on Partnering as a Strategy to Build a State-wide Network." *Medical Network Strategy Report,* 1997b, *6*(10), 1–3.

Enthoven, A. "There's Gold in Them Thar' Coalitions." *Managed Health-care,* 1997, *10*(7), 21–24.

Freudenheim, M. "Wellpoint Shares Sink Despite Profit Gain." *New York Times,* Oct. 31, 1997, p. C2.

Ginsburg, P. B., and Pickreign, J. D. "Tracking Health Care Costs: An Update." Cited in *Medical Benefits,* 1997, *14*(17), 7.

Goldman, E. F., and Corrigan, K. V. "'Thinking Retail' in Healthcare: New Approaches for Business Growth." *Healthcare Strategist,* 1997, *1*(1), 1–9.

Greene, J. "1997 Leadership Survey." Cited in *Medical Benefits,* 1997, *14*(17), 8.

Hamer, R. L. "HMO Facts and Trends." Presentation materials. St. Paul, Minn.: InterStudy, 1997a.

Hamer, R. L. "HMO Regional Market Analysis." *InterStudy Competitive Edge,* 1997b, *7*(2), 1–138.

Hamer, R. L. "Small Markets Present Opportunities for Provider-Sponsored Networks." Cited in *Healthcare Leadership Review,* 1997c, *16*(9), 9.

Holm, C. E., and Zuza, D. J. "Positioning Primary Care Networks: Understand What Managed Care Organizations Really Want." *Health Care Services Strategic Management,* 1997, *15*(8), 1, 22–23.

Hornung, K. "Tap into Patient Data to Bolster Your Disease Management Program." *Healthcare Demand & Disease Management,* 1997, *3*(7), 97–101.

"Hospital to Test Use of Computer-Based Reminders." *Health Data Network News,* 1997, *6*(10), 5, 7.

Japsen, B. "Survey: Money, Not Mission, Driving Mergers." *Modern Healthcare,* 1997, *27*(41), 14.

Kilborn, P. T. "Health Care Plans Are Seen Entering Rocky New Phase." *New York Times,* Nov. 22, 1997, pp. A1, A11.

Lagnado, L. "Ousted CEO of Columbia Leads Cable Buy." *Wall Street Journal,* Nov. 12, 1997, p. B10.

Lohr, S. "Information Technology Field Is Rated Largest U.S. Industry." *New York Times,* Nov. 18, 1997, p. C12.

Lowes, R. L. "The Second-Generation IPA: Will It Save Independent Practice?" *Medical Economics,* 1997, *74*(16), 182–191.

McGuire, J. "HMOs Expect Significant Premium Hikes for 1998." *Managed Care Outlook,* 1997, *10*(20), 7.

Meyer, H. "Beyond HMOs: The Tide of the Times." *Hospitals & Health Networks,* 1996, *70*(8), 34–40.

Monroe, S. "Health Care Merger and Acquisition Report." New Canaan, Conn.: Irving Lewis Associates. Cited in "Mergers: The Center of the Storm." *Hospitals & Health Networks,* 1996, *70*(8), 10.

Montague, J. "Mind over Maladies." *Hospitals & Health Networks,* 1996, *70*(8), 26–27.

Montague, J., and Pitman, H. "Currents: Information Systems." *Hospitals & Health Networks,* 1996, *70*(8), 10–11.

Peterson, S. "Can the New Medicine Heal You?" *D,* Nov. 1997, pp. 80–91.

Pinto, C. "1997 Design Awards." *Modern Healthcare,* 1997, *27*(41), 47–62.

Rodrigue, G. "Panel Calls for HMO Changes." *Dallas Morning News,* Nov. 20, 1997, pp. A1, A12.

Sharpe, A. "Columbia/HCA Weighs Plan to Spin Off One-Third of Company's 340 Hospitals." *Wall Street Journal,* Nov. 11, 1997, p. B13.

Slepin, R. E. "EDI Translates into Big Savings." *California HFMA Journal,* 1996, *9*(4), 48–49.

Walker, T. "Kaiser Poll Pans For-Profit Plans." *Managed Care,* 1997, *10*(7), 8.

Wall, P. "Consolidations Accelerate, Nearly Double in 1996." *California HFMA Journal,* 1997, *10*(1), 34–36.

Ward, T. *Co-Opetition: An Innovative Strategy Which Combines Cooperation and Competition.* Houston, Tex.: Ward Group, Oct. 1997.

Wechsler, J. "Proposal Struggles with Privacy and Practicality." *Managed Healthcare,* 1997, *7*(10), 15–16.

White, J. B., and Lagnado, L. "Columbia/HCA Dealt Sharp Blow by CalPERS Move." *Wall Street Journal,* Oct. 21, 1997, p. B5.

Woodyard, C., and Findlay, S. "Columbia to Dump a Third of Hospitals." *USA Today,* Nov. 18, 1997, p. B1.

Rural Health Systems

Jon B. Christianson
Anthony L. Wellever

Jon B. Christianson is a professor at the Institute for
Health Services Research at the University of Minnesota
School of Public Health. An economist who teaches,
researches, and writes about medical care financing
and evaluation, he has collaborated with health care
providers to evaluate new treatments. He is a member
of the editorial boards of Health Affairs and Medical
Care Research and Review and the coauthor of a paper
that won the 1995 Health Care Research Award of the
National Institute for Health Care Management.

Anthony L. Wellever is a research fellow and deputy
director of the Rural Health Research Center at the
University of Minnesota. He is the author or coauthor
of a number of articles about his research interests:
rural health networks, managed care in rural areas,
and alternative models for rural hospitals.

$\mathcal{A}$pproximately one in four Americans lives in a rural area. In the past, rural populations were defined by their dependence on farming and by their differences from urban populations in family size, lifestyle, and politics. Today, clear distinctions between urban and rural populations no longer exist. Sweeping improvements in transportation and communications, migration both to and from rural areas, and diversification of the rural economy have replaced simple definitions of rural with the concept that both rural and urban areas exist along a geographical continuum (Hewitt, 1992).

Rural areas are commonly associated with such geographical characteristics as small population, low population density, and isolation from urban centers. They also may be defined by economic and sociodemographic characteristics of the populations that inhabit rural areas. Meade (1992) combines geographical, economic, and socio-demographic characteristics to reach this broad definition of rural: "It encompasses farm and nonfarm, lands contiguous to great metropolises and lands remote from any town, places of economic growth and those of decline, places of retirement and those of abandonment. Such differences are associated with differences in demographic structure, that is, the proportion of different ages, races, and sexes. Because age, race, and sex are characterized by different levels of risk of various morbidity or mortality conditions, great variation in need for services in 'rural' America exists" (p. 69).

It is no longer possible to talk about rural America as a monolithic unit. Rural populations vary widely, leading to differing needs for health services. Education, income, occupation, political orientation, and physical isolation are among the many variables that might affect the need for health care services and the actions taken and causes supported to obtain services.

Rural populations are also volatile, shrinking and expanding in response to economic and social changes. Reversing the trend of the 1980s, when rural America suffered a net loss of 1.4 million residents, in the 1990s (through 1996) it witnessed a 2 million person net increase in population, with 75 percent of rural counties reporting population increases. The counties with the largest upswings are those with retirement or recreational facilities or those in proximity to a major population center (Cook, 1997). At the same time, some rural areas are virtually withering away. According to the 1990 Census, twenty-four rural counties, concentrated primarily in the Great Plains, lost sufficient population between 1980 and 1990 to gain *frontier* status (frontier counties are those with a population of six or fewer persons per square mile).

Out of this turbulent environment several population subgroups are emerging as particularly important as potential rural health care followers.

Uninsured Rural Residents

Some predominantly rural industries provide limited, if any, health insurance benefits to their employees. For example agriculture, forestry, and fishing provide health insurance coverage for approximately 40 percent of their workers and workers' families. Mining (also a rural industry but, unlike the others, one that is highly unionized) provides coverage to over 80 percent of its workers and their families. Approximately 96 percent of rural residents over age sixty-five are covered by Medicare and 5.8 percent of all rural residents are covered by public assistance programs, including Medicaid. Overall, 17.4 percent of rural residents have no health insurance (Office of Technology Assessment, 1990). The amount of out-of-pocket expense rural residents incur for health care is likely to influence their attitudes toward the health care system and the health care positions they support.

Rural Residents Enrolled in Managed Care

Medicare and Medicaid patients in rural areas likely will be channeled into managed care programs in increasing numbers in the future. Although Medicare managed care enrollment in rural areas is currently low (0.7 percent compared to the urban rate of 10.8 percent), recent changes in the method of payment for risk contractors serving rural areas almost ensure a significant increase in rural enrollment in the near future (Moscovice, Casey, and Krein, 1997). A majority of states are also preparing to embark on extending Medicaid managed care to rural areas.

Private managed care enrollment in rural areas also appears currently to lag substantially behind urban enrollment. Moreover, the high costs of marketing in rural areas, the small populations, and the lack of large employers suggest that private managed care enrollment may not develop as quickly in rural areas as publicly financed managed care enrollment. As a larger proportion of the elderly and poor are covered by managed care programs, conflicts may arise between these residents and rural providers over levels of payment and access to services.

Old and Young Rural Residents

For many years, better-educated young people have left rural areas. One explanation for their flight is that older residents control the wealth and land in rural areas, limiting young people's opportunities to participate in business or farming and causing them to seek opportunities elsewhere (Cook, 1997). This so-called brain drain is often lamented for its impact on the quality of rural leadership, but it also affects the ranks of followers. The young people who remain are less well off and less educated than other rural residents. They have substantial health care and social needs, but in comparison to their neighbors they may be less able or willing to mobilize behind community leaders to make their needs known. The elderly, in contrast, often have time to spend in community activities and the life experience to know how to accomplish their goals (Hobbs, 1997).

New Rural Residents

There are two general categories of new rural residents, the elderly seeking a safe, attractive, affordable retirement destination and young professionals seeking to improve the quality of their lives in, often idealistically envisioned, rural settings (Pooley, 1997). These newcomers frequently are more affluent than the established residents and have had their health care desires and expectations shaped by urban experiences. In some rural communities, clashes have resulted when *old-timers* perceived that newcomers were attempting to impose their cultural values upon them and the community at large. Many newcomers judge the quality and direction of rural social institutions such as schools, civic organizations, and hospitals as lacking and seek to reform them according to more urban standards, often meeting with resistance from long-time residents. Many key health care providers such as physicians and health services administrators have immigrated into rural communities from elsewhere.

These population subgroups implicitly and explicitly establish health care goals and select leaders. Conflicts among these goals are likely to become apparent as subgroups pursue them. How these conflicts are resolved is, in part, the job of leaders.

GOALS: LINKING FOLLOWERS AND LEADERS

Goals link followers and leaders. Burns (1978) observed that "persons are often perceived to be leaders simply because they reflect the needs and attitudes of their followers" (p. 265). Goals equalize leaders and followers: followers do not submit to a leader as a person but agree to join that leader in the common pursuit of a goal (Wills, 1994). Goals also serve as standards to evaluate policies, practices, other goals, and even leader performance. The performance of leaders is assessed by their contribution to change, as measured by goal attainment. Goals, then, are the principle organizing components of leadership: they bring followers and leaders together, direct their joint actions, and form the basis for evaluating leader performance (Burns, 1978).

Health care goals are formed by a variety of individual aspirations: economic (for example, a wish to lower expenditures or increase income), spiritual (for example, a desire for respect and dignity), and personal (for example, the hope of relieving one's own or a loved person's suffering). These individual desires find expression as the goals of a group, a community of interest. The goals of a particular group, however, are not static. They may change as intermediate steps are taken to attain them. As an interest group becomes larger, its goals may also become more diffuse or more grandiose. A larger group also faces the possibility of internal conflict that results in a modification of its original goals (Burns, 1978).

Rural areas' health care goals are numerous and vary widely from community to community. The population diversity described previously conveys to some degree the possible range of these health care goals. Examples of the likely goals of emerging subgroups are greater access to health care services (the uninsured and underinsured); lower out-of-pocket expenses and greater freedom of choice of providers (the insured); maintenance of local control of rural health care services (the *ruling elites*); and local access to a wider variety of health-related services and products (newcomers accustomed to the greater choices available in urban areas).

The various health-related interest groups in rural areas and the different goals they embrace provide many opportunities for the development of health care leaders.

LEADERS: WHO WILL LEAD?

Many different health care interest groups exist in rural areas, but each interest is not represented by a leader in every community. The lack of leadership to better define goals and to formulate and take actions to attain goals may result from a sense of powerlessness among followers in a community, a lack of information about possible courses of action, a lack of leadership ability, or the dominance of other issues.

Because many issues command rural residents' attention, health care goals are pursued by local leaders only to the extent that they are not eclipsed by other goals judged more immediate by leaders and followers. Health leadership, however, may be awakened by a catalytic event, or the perception of an impending catalytic event, such as the closure of a hospital service or an entire hospital, the loss of physicians to below the number acceptable to residents, the acquisition of local health care assets by interests outside of the community, or community awareness of a significant health care quality problem. For example, citing declining admissions and emergency room volume, the not-for-profit system that owned the hospital in Smithville, Missouri, converted the hospital to a skilled nursing facility. Community leaders emerged who attempted to gain ownership of the hospital through eminent domain. The not-for-profit system reopened the emergency room and is reevaluating its decision to close the acute care beds (Scott, 1997). Catalytic events are not only negative occurrences. A positive catalytic event, for example, would be the new availability of grant monies for community-based health planning.

When leaders emerge in rural areas, they typically adopt one of two leadership roles. They function either as specialized leaders, taking a narrow, subject-dominated view of community affairs, or as generalized leaders, expressing and coordinating a broad range of community interests. Specialized leaders, on the one hand, perform important community functions. They carry out task-oriented leadership activities that focus on the accomplishment of specific follower goals. Economic development, education, and recreation matters, for example,

80

benefit from specialized leadership and so do local health issues. Specialized leadership, however, can lead to fragmentation when the special interests of the group are viewed as greater than the interests of the community as a whole. Generalized leaders, on the other hand, fill structure-oriented leadership roles aimed at coordinating and integrating the goals of various special interest groups for the benefit of the entire rural community (Israel and Beaulieu, 1990).

Health care leadership in rural areas often is dominated by specialized leaders. Health care providers, health care facility trustees, and large employers frequently form the cadre of rural health leaders. They lend their clinical, administrative, and political expertise to planning, organizing, and controlling the local health care system. This is an appropriate role. Their leadership becomes counterproductive, however, when these leaders' and groups' private interests are pursued over the public interests of the greater community or when their goals are not or cannot be integrated with community goals. In the former case they benefit one segment of the community at the expense of others. In the latter case their specialized goal may serve multiple segments of the community, but failure to integrate the goal into the political and economic fabric of the entire community may undermine the community's overall effectiveness.

Rural health care providers, large employers, and health facility trustees may pursue goals particular to their occupational or fiduciary role, unaware of the possible negative consequences for other segments of the community or for the community at large. For example, a local manufacturing plant manager's primary health care goal may be to control premium prices, and that manager may be unaware or unconcerned about the consequences of her actions on the local availability of services or local health care provider income; local physicians motivated by the goal of maintaining their income may argue against the recruitment of needed additional health care providers; or a hospital trustee may lead a fund drive to keep the local hospital open even though it is underused, another hospital is located less than twenty miles away, and it requires a continuing subsidy from county tax revenues.

Individuals outside the community also provide rural health care leadership. In an effort to maintain or increase their market share, urban providers and health plans recently have accelerated a trend, begun in the mid-1980s, to expand their influence in rural areas. Their strategies include forming strategic alliances with existing rural

81

providers, offering previously unavailable health services locally, and competing with local providers within the rural community. One example of this trend is a clinical oncology outreach program at rural Kershaw County Memorial Hospital, offered in partnership with Richland Memorial Hospital in Columbia, South Carolina. Administrative staff, nursing administrators, medical staff, and pharmacists from both hospitals developed this chemotherapy clinic at Kershaw. The planning committee that directed the joint effort decided that the clinic would initially treat relatively stable patients using routine protocols but that patients requiring radiation therapy would still travel to Columbia. Richland Memorial made available its clinical and planning expertise to provide a previously unavailable service to Kershaw County, and it benefits from this arrangement by receiving referrals from Kershaw County (Moscovice and others, 1995).

Outside influence on local health care systems is a highly contentious issue. There are segments of rural communities that welcome the expansion of urban health care providers and plans into rural areas, in the belief that access to services will improve, facilities will be upgraded, and quality of care will be enhanced. Others view the increased presence of urban health care providers and plans as a challenge to local control of health care services and doubt the long-term strength of the urban commitment to rural health. For example, in the Smithville example cited earlier, the not-for-profit system owner closed the hospital when it was no longer profitable to operate. Whether or not they currently hold title to the hospital, many rural residents believe that they still *own* it. "We started the community hospital," a local leader in Smithville is reported to have said, and indeed, many rural hospitals would not exist but for the efforts of the parents and grandparents of current rural residents (Scott, 1997). Whether or not urban health care providers and plans maintain their interest in rural health care in the future, for the time being they are likely to have an impact on health care leadership in many rural communities.

These "outsiders" may serve as catalysts, encouraging the development of local leaders to support or oppose their presence in the community. Nevertheless, some local health care decisions will now be made by individuals residing outside the rural community. Effective community leadership may ameliorate the potential negative consequences of this external decision making by developing agreements with urban health care providers and plans that outline a role for the community in decisions that affect its well-being. In the anecdotal evidence that exists to date, there is little to suggest that urban health care providers and plans adopt a public-be-damned attitude when they enter rural areas. On the contrary, to the extent that they are made aware of rural residents' needs, desires, and values, they attempt to incorporate these issues into their business plans. They are, after all, in the business of selling products and services in a competitive market, and aggressive disregard for consumers is not a useful marketing strategy.

The health care system in many rural communities for the foreseeable future will feature a mixture of local and extralocal ownership of health care resources. Effective rural health care leaders will attempt to find ways that these interests can coexist and will avoid exploiting their differences for the particular benefit of a narrow segment of the rural community.

THE FUTURE OF RURAL HEALTH LEADERSHIP

It is common for rural health advocates to lament the lack of health care leadership in rural communities (Amundson, 1993; Amundson and Rosenblatt, 1991). In the past decade, private philanthropic organizations such as the Kellogg Foundation, the Northwest Area Foundation, the Colorado Trust, and the Kansas Health Foundation have sought to correct this situation by investing considerable effort and money in programs to develop rural community health care leadership. These programs have encouraged grant communities to organize themselves into broadly representative community bodies, select leaders, assess community health care needs, develop plans to address identified needs, and implement projects designed by community leaders. The communities that participated in these programs benefited not only from the grant dollars that flowed into the community but also from the outside technical expertise provided directly by the foundations or by consultants funded through the grants. In some cases the technical assistance took the form of leadership development. In other cases consultants played the role of knowledgeable but disinterested parties who were able to bridge gaps among special interests and focus attention on the entire community. Despite the programs' usefulness and the sums of money spent on them, the number of communities that received grant support was relatively small.

The vast majority of rural communities have received neither grant money nor technical assistance from outside the community to address local health care issues.

A growing body of research examines the characteristics of *effective* rural communities. Findings from this research indicate that the communities best able to act on local concerns have leaders skilled in involving a diverse set of actors in local decision-making activities, operate on democratic principles, and place the welfare of the whole community above the needs of any special interest (Israel and Beaulieu, 1990). The research goes on to show that these communities not only make better use of their own resources but are also better able to identify and use specialized outside resources. According to these studies, the most effective rural leaders are those who participate in networks beyond their communities (Hobbs, 1997).

These findings seem to suggest that the most successful rural health care leaders view health care in a broad social context. This is not to say there is no role for specialized leaders, but to be truly effective, they must pursue the interests of the public at large and be able to coordinate and integrate community health care decisions with the interests of other specialized leaders in the community.

The interest urban providers and plans have in rural areas may have a beneficial effect on rural health care leadership. On the one hand the entry or anticipated entry of an urban provider or plan may catalyze the development of local leaders. On the other hand, if local leaders reach out to the urban interests, they may find technical and financial resources equivalent to those provided by philanthropic foundations. What is viewed by many as the loss of local control of rural health may result in a revitalization of local health care leadership.

References

Amundson, B. "Myth and Reality in the Rural Health Services Crisis: Facing Up to Community Responsibilities." *Journal of Rural Health,* 1993, *9*(3), 179–187.

Amundson, B., and Rosenblatt, R. "The WAMI Rural Hospital Project: Overview and Conclusions." *Journal of Rural Health,* 1991, *7*(5), 560–574.

Burns, J. M. *Leadership.* New York: HarperCollins, 1978.

Cook, R. "America's Heartland: Neither One Mind Nor One Heart." *Congressional Quarterly,* Sept. 20, 1997, pp. 2243–2249.

Hewitt, M. "Defining 'Rural' Areas: Impact on Health Care Policy and Research." In W. M. Gesler and T. C. Rickets (eds.), *Health in North America: The Geography of Health Care Services and Delivery.* New Brunswick, N.J.: Rutgers University Press, 1992.

Hobbs, D. "The Context of Rising Rates of Rural Violence and Substance Abuse: The Problems and Potential of Rural Communities." [http://www.ncrel.org/sdrs/areas/issues/envrmnt/drugfree/v1hobbs2.htm]. Feb. 28, 1997.

Israel, G., and Beaulieu, L. "Community Leadership." In A. Luloff and L. Swanson (eds.), *American Rural Communities.* Boulder, Colo.: Westview Press, 1990.

Meade, M. S. "Implications of Changing Demographic Structures for Rural Health Services." In W. M. Gesler and T. C. Rickets (eds.), *Health in North America: The Geography of Health Care Services and Delivery.* New Brunswick, N.J.: Rutgers University Press, 1992.

Moscovice, I., Casey, M., and Krein, S. *Rural Managed Care: Patterns & Prospects.* Minneapolis, Minn.: Rural Health Research Center, Division of Health Services Research and Policy, School of Public Health, University of Minnesota, Apr. 1997.

Moscovice, I. J., and others. *Building Rural Hospital Networks.* Ann Arbor, Mich.: Health Administration Press, 1995.

Office of Technology Assessment. *Health Care in Rural America.* OTA-H-434. Washington, D.C.: U.S. Government Printing Office, 1990.

Pooley, E. "The Great Escape." *Time,* Dec. 8, 1997, pp. 52–65.

Scott, L. "Communities Strike Back: Residents Oppose Ceding Control to Outside Not-for-Profit Chains." *Modern Healthcare,* 1997, *27*(17), 26–32.

Wills, G. *Certain Trumpets: The Call of Leaders.* New York: Simon & Schuster, 1994.

86

SECTION THREE

*Succeeding in a Market-Driven
Environment: A Case Study*

Succeeding in a Market-Driven Environment: A Case Study

Julianne M. Morath, MS, RN

Abbott Northwestern Hospital, a large, tertiary care center located in Minneapolis, is typical of hospitals nationwide that are learning to provide care to patients and families in a market-driven environment. In the hospital's effort to apply a business mentality to its system of care delivery, its care providers, in particular, have had to overcome concerns over compromising professional values and standards.

This chapter focuses on the success of Abbott Northwestern's nursing department in making the transition to delivering care in a market-driven environment. In addition to describing the nursing department's journey, the chapter highlights some of the innovative programs that have resulted from the change process. An appendix at the back of the chapter condenses some of the requirements for practice in the new business environment.

The Movement of Business into Health Care: Background

In the past 10 years, employer demands, the move to capitation, and a significant reduction in the demand for certain health care services all have led to the development of large, integrated systems across the country, including in the Twin Cities and surrounding regions. Today, the health care market in the Twin Cities is characterized by:

The author would like to acknowledge these individuals for their spirit, expertise, and leadership: Mary Koloroutis; Carol Huttner; Ann Watkins; Ruth Sohl-Krieger; Pat Hartwig; Elaine Slocumb; Monica Sieg; Marjean Leary; Elaine Hogan-Miller; Phyllis Collier; Ginger Malone; Marge Watry; Terry Voigt; Audrey Haag; Robert K. Spinner; Todd Miller, MD; Sarah Horsman; Debra Waggoner; Deidre Perkins; and Nancy Garner Ebert. The author also would like to acknowledge the nurses, physicians, and employees at Abbott Northwestern Hospital for their work that created the content of this chapter.

- The alignment of insurers with providers, and physician practices with hospitals
- An increased number of physician group practices, physician–hospital organizations, and system-owned practices
- Increased opportunities for providers such as nurse practitioners, wellness and health specialists, and chiropractors, among others
- Increased cooperation in the area of technology among institutions
- The issue of excess hospital bed capacity

As a result, in their attempts to provide care, health care institutions in the Twin Cities are faced with:

- Continued provider integration and shrinkage in the inpatient market
- More and stronger competition for inpatient care and specialty referrals
- Greater accountability for the community's health
- Increased system emphasis on clinical integration and efficiency
- Larger and more assertive buyer coalitions
- Continued focus on primary care as the center of health care delivery
- Continued proliferation of technology at a time when rationalization and regionalization have become survival strategies
- Stagnating federal and state health reform (although the reform of integrated delivery systems continues to progress)

The purchasers of health care are clear about their needs: predictable, stable, affordable prices; elimination of what they perceive as unnecessary and inappropriate care; a network of convenient primary care and specialty providers; and data to support continued value improvement in health care, especially in outcome research.[1]

Making the transition from a patient-driven to a market-driven health care system requires hospitals to make significant shifts in thinking and to acquire a business orientation. It requires that hospitals move from knowing what they think is best for their customers to learning what their customers require of them. It requires care providers to shift from making decisions independently to making decisions interdependently. This new business orientation means moving beyond relying on routines, rituals, and individual preferences to providing data-based care and searching for the best practice, from complex system messes to simplified processes and systems that fulfill customer needs; from giving everything to the patient to providing the patient with the best value (defined as the best cost and quality outcome), with service quality as the distinguishing advantage.

The movement of business into health care has produced integrated networks that align the incentives and services of providers, delivery systems, and health plans into a single organization. Their combined focus is on cost reduction, process improvement, and value creation. The integrated service network model first surfaced in 1962 when Alfred Dupont Chandler, historian of business at the Harvard Business School, suggested that when manufacturing systems were integrated, the resulting cost and service advantages would enable those businesses to dominate their industry.[2]

In the health care industry, similar realignments will satisfy a number of purposes, including:

- Creating an integrated system
- Accepting a single check from a public or private sponsor for an enrolled population
- Using the resulting pool of funds to cover the health needs of that population
- Ensuring that everyone involved in the care of that population gets paid

All this, it is believed, will be easier to do if the pieces of the system are integrated and owned or employed by a single organization. Does this type of integration work in health care? The jury is still out.[3]

The Transition at Abbott Northwestern Hospital

At Abbott Northwestern Hospital, the transition to a stronger business orientation is well under way. The hospital is now part of Allina, an integrated service network whose name connotes alignment. Allina brings together providers, delivery sites, and insurance products. As part of an integrated service network, the system's measure of success is changing from *patients* to *covered lives*. Hospitals are viewed as expense centers, and their use of resources must be contained or reduced. In the new system, the site of care is increasingly being relocated to home, community, nursing home, school, and other less-intensive, less-invasive settings. (Futurists predict that within this decade, 80 percent of the procedures currently being performed in hospital main operating rooms will be relocated to outpatient settings.) Abbott Northwestern's licensed capacity of 900 beds was often full. Today, the operating capacity is 500 beds with a fluctuating census. Length of stay (LOS) is 5.2 days, and intensity of care is increasing steadily.

Care Documentation

As the hospital moves toward a stronger business orientation, employers are requiring documentation of the plan to organize, sequence, and deliver care and services for case types—a *care pathway* or documented process of care. The business world has used process identification and measurement since Walter Shewhart of Bell Laboratories introduced the concept of the control chart, a simple but powerful tool of business measurement.[4] Today, health care organizations are beginning to identify care processes and key organizational or support processes and place them in control. Historically, health care organizations have been organized around departments or professions as they serve patients. The identification of processes across traditional boundaries and points of disconnection provides the opportunity for integration that will eliminate duplication, competition, and fragmentation.

At Abbott Northwestern, the key processes identified in the plan for patient care are:

- Wellness and prevention
- Assessment and diagnosis
- Intervention and therapy
- Caring and relating

The last process in the preceding list reflects the personal and therapeutic dimensions of the relationships involved in health care. Support processes include accessing, planning, documenting, coordinating, information processing, educating, resource allocating, and monitoring. (See figure 1)

The Documentation Tool

In nursing care delivery, the primary documentation tool is the care pathway, which stabilizes and documents the process of care by diagnosis-related group (DRG), reflecting the interdisciplinary collaboration required to implement care for a defined population. *Care pathways* are the clinical processes—the specific practices in the delivery of patient care for a specific case type—that guide the sequencing, coordination, and detailing of specific elements of the care process. They are used to track costs and identify trends. When these care processes are stabilized, they can be measured and improved. The compression of variance and identification of best practice is a focus.

In the acute care setting, a variance committee measures deviation from the expected pathway. (*Variance* is the measure of deviation between what happened and what was expected to happen during a patient's care.) This measure provides meaningful information that can be used to evaluate the care processes and identify improvement opportunities. Variance studies focus on the key events identified by a multidisciplinary team during pathway design. The variance data can be used to improve the care of a specific patient to either continually advance his or her progress or reassess the plan for care.

Variance from a pathway also can be analyzed for a group of patients, and a pathway thus becomes a tool that supports quality improvement and outcome measurement. A pathway variance study begins by focusing the patient population. The principle of *leverage,* or determining where the greatest impact can be made, is used. Things to consider when determining the patient population include the top DRG list, quality reports, satisfaction

Figure 1. **Patient Care Delivery Model**

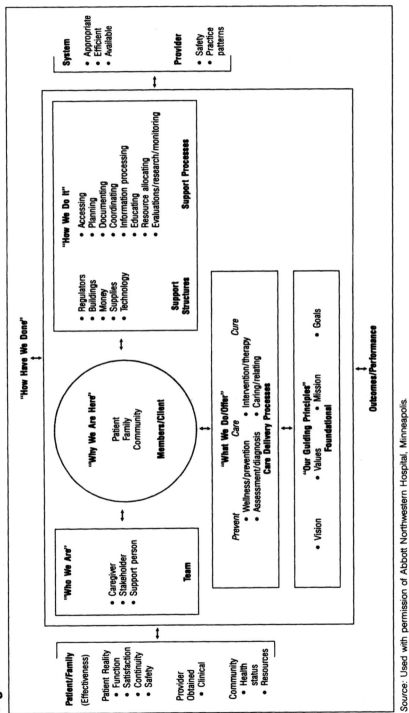

Source: Used with permission of Abbott Northwestern Hospital, Minneapolis.

91

surveys, populations at risk, outcome management strategies, or studies in process. The study team determines the sample size and time frame needed to collect the data. Data collection can be done through concurrent input of data or retrospective review. Data are analyzed by a variety of possible resources, including pathway development groups, patient care councils, quality management staff, and those involved in continuous quality improvement (CQI) projects. Findings are communicated, and plans for improvement are made by identifying the potential explanations for the identified variance. Assessment is made as to whether the explanation was valid, findings are documented, data are analyzed, and interventions are made by modifying or changing the process of care. Finally, the variance study efforts are evaluated, and the need for further study to evaluate the effectiveness of the intervention is identified.

Following are examples of how pathway variance studies were used at Abbott Northwestern and their results:

- One study undertaken by the neuroscience division to evaluate the microdiscectomy pathway showed that 83 percent of patients had a variance in pain management. A multidisciplinary team consisting of neurosurgeons, nurses, and a pharmacist analyzed medication-specific data and other pain interventions for these patients. Based on data from the analysis, the team incorporated Agency for Health Care Policy and Research (AHCPR) guidelines on acute pain management into the pathway, including generic postoperative orders. Follow-up variance data have shown that only 19 percent of patients now have pain as a variance, an improvement of 64 percent. The reduction in variance has resulted in improved patient care, reduced LOS, and reduced charges.[6]
- With bypass surgery patients reporting that the single worst aspect of their procedure was having the endotracheal tube in so long after surgery, the bypass surgery value enhancement team decided to draft clinical criteria for tube removal. The result was that in only three years, early extubation increased from just 2 to 58 percent. Not only can patients now move more freely and communicate with their families, but there has been a decrease in infection rate, a reduction in the amount of sedation required, and a full-day reduction in LOS in the intensive care unit.

The hospital now is in the process of attaching supply utilization to the care pathway with the intention of isolating and measuring resources and costs. It is conceivable that this could lead to a preferred supplier system in which a supplier with a demonstrable quality program, best cost, and willingness to enter into a long-term relationship and share risk in capitation is selected to work exclusively with the hospital. This requires measurement and joint monitoring of utilization, quality, and cost trends.

The Impact of Business Science on the Art of Caring

When considering how business science will affect care delivery, one question that arises is: Can the processes of care truly be standardized? Unlike the manufacturing process, variability in the human response to illness creates variability in individual expressions of disease. For example, people may express their illnesses and respond to interventions in markedly distinctive ways based on their level of knowledge about their illness, their history, their level of anxiety, and the presence or absence of a support system.

The relationship between members of the clinical community and patients/families is unique and based on individualized requirements. As patients/families become the clinical community's partners in care, the hospital's ability to execute the process of care to meet the unique requirements of the individual will be the distinguishing advantage for providers and organizations. This is thought of as management of the patient/family experience of care.

A reductionistic and mechanistic application of business science in health care without use of the art of caring can be limiting. The danger exists that this would diminish the caring and relating processes of the hospital's work. At the center of this work is an intentional caring that creates the safety necessary for healing, empowerment, and growth. This caring is intimate and personal, and is not expressed in a case-specific care pathway or process.

Can discipline be applied to this intentional caring? The answer is yes, through the measurement of sentient quality. *Quality,* a word that is read, spoken, and heard daily in health care today, has two dimensions of emphasis. These are best defined in Gerteis's book *Through the Patient's Eyes,* which describes the Picker-Commonwealth study of patient satisfaction.[7]

One dimension has to do with technical excellence. This includes professional skill and competence, and the capacity of diagnostic and therapeutic equipment, procedures, and systems to accomplish what they are meant to accomplish reliably and effectively in a way that is readily measurable and quantifiable.

The second dimension is more difficult to measure but cannot be diminished or ignored. It relates to the texture and substance of personal experience, and sometimes is referred to as *sentient quality*—the quality of a sensation and experience or the quality of a human relationship. It is in this dimension of caring that true healing occurs, because it is this dimension that patients/families experience most directly. Gerteis aptly describes how this dimension influences patient/family perceptions of safety and well-being, responses to illness, and feelings of receiving care. Patients/families develop these perceptions through interactions with professional providers, observations of providers' interactions with each other, and experiences in the settings in which services are provided.

Today, health care providers face unyielding issues of access, cost, and clinical effectiveness. Especially now, they must be ever aware of the experiential dimension of their practice. Providers know that patients want and need an enhanced sense of well-being that incorporates respect, choice, privacy, safety, and relief from the effects of illness. A therapeutic relationship, no matter how brief, affords the opportunity for true caring and healing to take place, thus allowing the artistry and the science of health care to be practiced simultaneously to achieve quality of care.

Some aspects of the patient/customer requirements described in the Picker-Commonwealth study can be met through deliberate, disciplined approaches to care and by placing a process in control, such as systematic implementation of AHCPR pain guidelines. However, other aspects of care, such as respect, depend on the quality of relationships established among unique individuals based on assessment of need and understanding of the caring phenomenon.

Is the use of business systems diminishing the care provided to patients? Today, patients are asking more from hospitals than they have been given previously. For example, they are asking for cost and quality outcomes. They are requiring seamless, integrated care that is communicated to them clearly and in which they can participate. And they are requiring access to service and service quality. Responding to customer requirements is both good business and good care.

References to business systems often highlight only the production model of business. This focus does not recognize that around half of today's business systems produce services. Business consists of both service and production. Hospitals, clinics, and other health care organizations have much in common with service business models. For example, practices related to the hotel industry and business concepts such as expectation theory and purchase behavior clearly apply to the provision of health care services.

Making the transition to this market-driven environment in which business practices are used requires discipline, a grounding in professional practice that includes the patient/customer as a participant, and an organizational context to support the work. This begins with an intentional and systemic approach to change. The remainder of this chapter highlights the foundational work for that change in Abbott Northwestern Hospital's nursing department.

The Nursing Department's Journey of Change

Abbott Northwestern Hospital has been an engine of growth and financial success throughout its history. It was process oriented, with less emphasis on outcome. Its structure was decentralized with a traditional hierarchy that focused on discrete functional areas and multiple systems and processes that operated independently. This was not sustainable. Following is a description of how the transition to a market-driven mentality was accomplished within the hospital's nursing department.

Building the Vision

The nursing department's journey of change began firmly grounded in philosophy and vision. The department's philosophy was retested to act as a moral compass through the change process. It is based on advocacy through caring. The department's vision represents the shared vision of more than 300 nurses, each with a personal view of the ideal practice experience.

Personal visions were elicited from three sources:

1. Nurses who attended educational sessions entitled Advocacy through Caring
2. Nurses who attended retreats entitled Personal Mastery
3. Participants from ongoing focus groups with the nurse executive

The resultant vision was simple and powerful:

Patients are the reason we exist. People are the reason we excel. Systems support the work.

The complete version is provided in figure 2.

Assessing the Current Reality

An assessment of the current reality of nursing practice was conducted using the same three sources that helped build the department's vision, and a

Figure 2.   The Vision of the Nursing Department Abbott Northwestern Hospital

Practice—Patients are the reason we exist.

The philosophy of nursing is lived in practice every day by each nurse. Nurses practice their profession with confidence, compassion, and skill.

Relationships—People are the reason we excel.

Through our words and actions, nurses inspire, recognize, and reward leadership and expect care for the caregiver; and require professional development and collaborative governance.

Diversity in nursing is our strength. Our ability to collaborate brings our best to the patient and strengthens our profession. This strength and energy allow us to enter into collegial relationships that produce extraordinary results on behalf of our patients and the organization.

Systems—Systems support the work.

Nurses are wise stewards of resources and use the tools, methods, and technology of quality improvement and innovation to refine practice and influence the systems that affect it.

systematic inventory of the system of care delivery was conducted by the department's nurse leaders. The assessment resulted in a painful but candid reflection of the gap between vision and reality. This gap provided the energy for change.

A specific plan of operations was established to move the nursing organization toward its new vision. To show that patients were the reason the department existed, the plan recognized the need to identify patient-focused customer requirements. To show that people were the reason the department excelled, operational goals included creation of an informed, competent workforce with access to the necessary skills and support to learn and develop continuously. To create systems that supported the work, the plan reflected the department's aim to reduce complexity, identify and improve key processes, and redesign work and access to information. The plan focused the department's priorities and moved it toward outcome orientation.

More specifically, the three parts of the vision were embodied in the daily work of the nursing department in various ways. To develop the *patients are the reason we exist* part of the vision statement, the department focused on improving its ability to listen to customers. Patient surveys, focus groups, and patient participation in care delivery redesign were used to increase the department's knowledge of patient requirements and perceptions, and data resulting from these initiatives were used to create action plans to improve customer service and nurse responsiveness. Today, whenever tensions arise concerning a course of action, the question "What would the patient expect of us in this situation?" is used to consider and resolve the issue. The Personal Mastery retreat (described later in this chapter), a program to increase the capacity of employees to contribute to the success of the organization, was established to embody the value *people are the reason we excel. Systems support the work,* the third component of the vision, has been evidenced through the support of process improvement teams working on issues such as improving case cart completion in the operating room, simplifying and improving the patient registration process, and implementing a point-of-care computerized clinical documentation system for the intensive care unit.

Building a Supportive Structure

A new structure was needed to release the collective talent and intellect of the nursing department so that it could move toward its new vision. The first reorganization resulted in the notion of a matrix to (1) identify key processes that would provide an infrastructure to support, rather than direct, the work of nursing and patient care and (2) assign accountability for those processes. As figure 3 shows, the vertical axis represented program/operational responsibilities, and the horizontal axis introduced the emphasis on key processes that crossed all operational areas. These processes

Figure 3. Infrastructure Matrix That Supports the Work of Nursing at Abbott Northwestern Hospital

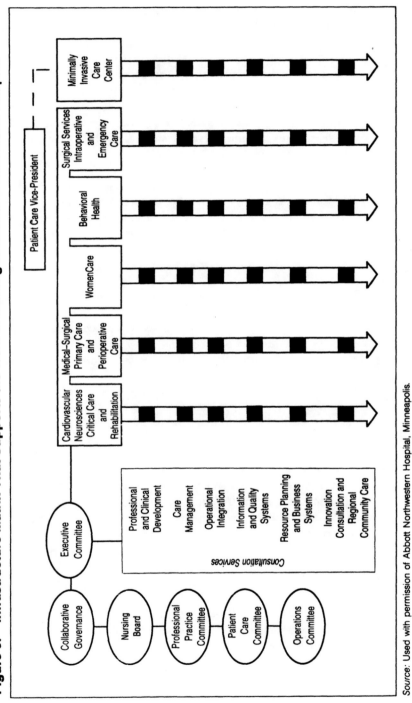

Source: Used with permission of Abbott Northwestern Hospital, Minneapolis.

included professional and clinical development; care management; operational integration or assurance of coordination across division boundaries; information and quality systems; resource planning and business systems; and innovation, consultation, and regional community care.

The structure was designed to support the functional areas and also to identify, strengthen, and manage the department's key processes—the infrastructure or foundation upon which care is delivered. Its intent was to create a leaner, more horizontal organization. The structure recognized the ability of nurses to be full partners in the governance of practice. It created an interdependence among nursing leaders, and the focus and alignment to end internal competition and duplication and to enhance collaboration. Its focus was on patients and care processes rather than on the departments and divisions in which care was delivered. This structure is reflected in the nursing department's collaborative governance structure, now four years old. An operations plan reflects the department's intention, and an implementation plan reflects its commitment to achieve its vision. Priorities for action and resources are established by the operations plan.

The nursing department structure had clear guiding principles:

- The department is integrating and aligning to support high-quality patient care.
- The structure is not hierarchical; nurses will function as a team for the benefit of the whole department.
- The structure supports department priorities to focus nursing's activities with an emphasis on outcomes.
- The structure is based on the principles of a learning organization, capitalizing on the collective strengths and talents of all members rather than on the skills of individual members.
- Communication will be key to the department's success. This includes not only communication between nurses but also between the nursing department and its various constituencies about what is and is not working.
- Concerns about changes will be discussed openly. If withheld, they will likely come out when it is too late to make a difference.
- Nurses cannot work as a team unless they are a team. This will necessitate a commitment of time, energy, and expertise.
- Nurses must be clear about the expected outcomes and be willing to set their course to achieve them.
- The vision must be clearly articulated and must include priorities.

The nurse director role was retitled nurse leader/consultant, and its responsibilities shifted from those of an advocate for a given department to those of a leader who would:

- Ensure the integration and alignment of the pieces to the whole organization

- Develop and implement strategic direction by engaging in strategic dialogue, by being the steward of the organization's resources, and by being the hospital's eyes and ears in anticipating change
- Create, lead, perpetuate, and sustain a shared vision, values, and culture
- Be a living example of quality principles such as mentoring, teaching, and stewardship
- Ensure that the organization has effective systems by identifying and validating them, devoting resources to their success, and evaluating them by determining whether they had a broad impact, were cost-effective, and facilitated achievement of intended outcomes
- Communicate with, be a resource for, consult with, and partner with others and the organization to solve problems
- Understand and respond to customer requirements and perceptions

Creating Communities of Care

The combined pressures of declining inpatient census and rising costs required greater flexibility and more facile movement of staffing and beds to meet changing requirements, which included census fluctuations as great as 20 percent in either direction within patient care units and the fact that distribution of patient population by specialty varied greatly. At the same time, the need for highly competent staff who were able to advance the plan of care was essential.

This dilemma led to the creation of communities of care. These patient-centered communities among units that share common elements gave staff and managers more flexibility in responding to changing requirements. The reorganization reduced management positions, improved relationships among patient care areas, built new partnerships, and reflected changes made by nurses through the collaborative governance process. Issues of "being pulled" or "floating" to another unit diminished as territories became less demarcated. Nurses were able to be more versatile in their practice. The communities of care created a new sense of "us," rather than the culture of "we and they" that sometimes exists between specialties. Examples of communities are medical–surgical care, cardiovascular care, orthoneuroscience-rehabilitative care, and WomenCare.

The word *community* was chosen carefully and deliberately, and was influenced by the work of Dr. M. Scott Peck.[8] It connotes a group of people committed to a common purpose and to each other. The notion of community transforms the interaction between nurse and hospital from a purely financial transaction (where the nurse's skills are purchased to complete work) to a collaborative effort in which both nurse and hospital serve a common purpose.

Within communities of care, nurse managers partner with each other in the provision of leadership, each with a different yet complementary focus.

These partnerships are formed of tough, compassionate, complementary-skilled managers committed to common goals. Peter Senge suggests that the essential component of a learning organization is the learning partnership two people can form when they are communicating and working together.[9] Such a partnership is unique and provides structure. Each individual brings to it a new way of interacting and feeling that facilitates commitment. It improves the quality of thinking and decision making, and models the essentials of learning for the community, councils, and work groups.

The partnership encourages managers to rid themselves of traditional approaches to managing or leading other people and to move toward empowerment and facilitation. They have not job-shared but have analyzed and distributed the work to become more effective. A computer local-area network system has created virtual centralization that gives access to real-time data to support decision making, information sharing, and learning.

The Results of the Journey

Over the course of two years, the nursing department's organizational structure matured to look like the model shown in figure 4-4. This model represents how nursing practice now works within the organizational structure of the hospital. Its emphasis is on the relationship of the nurses' work—and the means by which it is accomplished—to patients, rather than on reporting relationships among individuals. In the model, the work of the nursing department is defined by the requirements of the patient populations it serves. The areas of nursing governance and practice; process pathways; and clinical practice model standards, guidelines, and protocols are the responsibility of the nursing practice division. For figure 4, the following areas are included under the umbrella of wellness-prevention, episodic care, acute-rehabilitative care, and maintenance and chronic care:

- Clinical nurse specialist group practice
- Enterstomal nursing
- Emergency care
- Healthy communities
- Outreach
- Consultation
- WomenCare
- Medical/surgical care
- Minimally invasive care center
- Ambulatory care
- Surgical services
- Perioperative care
- Critical care

Figure 4. Patient Care: Nursing Services Component

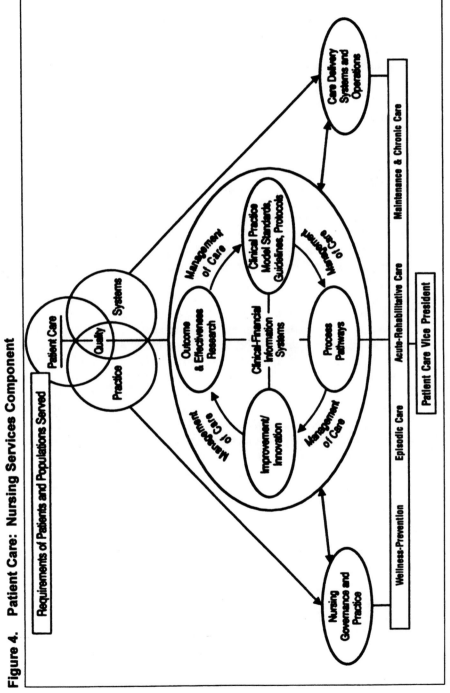

Source: Used with permission of Abbott Northwestern Hospital, Minneapolis.

- Cardiovascular–renal care
- Ortho–back–transitional care unit–neuro–rehab care
- Oncology
- Virginia Piper Cancer Institute care
- Behavioral health care

Three organizing principles—patient care, practice, and systems—described in the department's vision are used to structure the department's work:

1. *Patient care:* Patient care is the purpose of the department; in other words, it is the reason the department exists. Each member of the nursing department is responsible and accountable for patient care; this principle is the embodiment of nursing's philosophy and reflects its commitment to quality.

   Nursing care is data-based assessment, nursing diagnosis, planning, intervention, and evaluation of outcomes of care. Patient care requires that nursing care be integrated into the work of the care team, coordinating aspects of intervention and services required by patients/families across the continuum of care. The outcomes of patient care to be measured include patient, family, and community perception of function, health status, knowledge, safety, continuity, and satisfaction.

2. *Practice:* This is the domain that supports the work of patient care by ensuring that nurses and other direct or supportive caregivers and staff are appropriately licensed and that competencies based on standards of clinical practice are established, performances measured, competence ensured, and practice enhanced through continuing clinical and professional development. Practice outcomes to be measured include provider practice patterns, competency, safety, and meaningful work.

3. *Systems:* Systems include the methods, tools, procedures, and relationships that facilitate the work of patient care and integrate nursing into the whole of patient care delivery across the health care system. Patient flow, information transfer, communication, and cooperative relationships on a practical, daily basis depend on systems. Systems outcomes to be measured include the appropriateness, efficiency, and availability of resources.

The area of nursing governance and practice is the one in which the necessary nursing talent and expertise is coordinated to support practice capabilities and accountabilities. Care delivery systems and operations represent the coordination of leaders who support the systems of operations, resource allocation, and coordination and alignment of actions in the provision of patient care through the operations plan.

The Quality of Care Delivery

The principles of patient care, practice, and systems find integration through quality. *Quality* encompasses the mind-set, culture, theories, tools, and methods for continuously pursuing excellence that inspire vision and patient-focused care. In clinical nursing practice, quality is achieved through each individual's commitment to do the right thing, in the right way, at the right time, and in the right sequence to achieve reliable, predictable, and desired outcomes.

Quality also is each individual's willingness to work according to data-based standards, to be measured against those standards, and to be accountable for continuously improving performance. This work is achieved through:

- Use of the standards, guidelines, and protocols of the professional practice model
- Development and use of interdisciplinary pathways to guide the process of care
- Use of variance studies and other strategies to improve care and discover care innovations
- Use of research to add to nursing's knowledge and understanding of its work

The work of quality is supported through the collection, organization, integration, and analysis of clinical and financial data for decision making and learning.

The Continuum of Care Delivery

Care is provided according to care management strategies that recognize that there is a continuum in the patient experience that needs to be coordinated across delivery sites, geography, providers, services, and resources. Care and services are provided episodically in intervals from minutes to hours; in emergency, outpatient, minimally invasive care settings to acute, inpatient hospital settings; and over time in a variety of settings for maintenance, chronic, and hospice care. Increasingly, attention to wellness and prevention is emphasized in work with individuals, populations, and communities.

The Organization of Care Delivery

With attention to the continuum, the organization of care delivery is provided through the communities of care discussed earlier. Clinical nurse managers work in partnership to manage these communities and to provide practice leadership to achieve efficient and effective outcomes. Each community has a qualified nurse leader/consultant.

The administrative structure of the hospital is aligned so that the nurse leader/consultant works directly with administrators and physicians to plan, facilitate, evaluate, and enhance the program areas they represent. Nurse leaders/consultants have a direct, functional reporting relationship to the patient care vice-president (or to an operations vice-president), who is a qualified registered nurse executive, for professional standards of care and practice; for review of licensure and competence; and for access to consultation, decision making, care coordination, and educational and professional activities. The patient care vice-president provides clinical and administrative leadership and support, and is steward to the delivery of high-quality patient care and professional practice.

Innovations Supporting Organizational Change

Several key innovations made the restructuring of the nursing department possible. These included:

- The collaborative governance model
- The Advocacy through Caring program
- The Personal Mastery program

The Collaborative Governance Model

Collaborative governance is a communication and decision-making model that places the responsibility, authority, and accountability for nursing care with the practicing nurse. This is achieved through a clinical nursing structure that integrates with the management/administrative structure to create an environment of shared vision and excellence in patient care and nursing practice.

The model is implemented through a system of councils, committees, and a board, which have responsibility, accountability, and authority for conducting the business of the nursing department in the areas of strategic planning, development and evaluation, patient care, professional practice, and operational efficiency. The ongoing assessment of the functioning of collaborative governance is vital to its continued efficiency and effectiveness.

The collaborative governance model recognizes the knowledge, creativity, and talent of the clinical staff, and is recognized as a vehicle for bringing to daily practice the nursing philosophy and clinical practice model core beliefs.

The clinical structure of collaborative governance is based on these beliefs:

- Knowledge with participation is power.
- Given sufficient information, people will make appropriate decisions.

- Individuals are unique in their contributions.
- A sense of purpose, commitment, and optimal productivity results when organizational and personal goals are congruent.
- Risk taking, in itself, is growth.
- Differences are valued and offer the opportunity for learning.
- People are honest and trustworthy and will work hard to achieve their full potential.
- Individuals are accountable and responsible for their practice.
- Problems identified are mutually owned, and responsibility for resolution begins with problem identification.
- Collaboration with other departments and disciplines is essential to fulfill the hospital's mission.
- Individuals are empowered to meet their full potential.

The Advocacy through Caring Program

Advocacy through Caring is a major tenet of nursing department philosophy at Abbott Northwestern Hospital. The philosophy describes values and beliefs that are at the foundation of professional practice. The Advocacy through Caring program is planned for RNs during their first quarter of employment and for colleagues who want the opportunity to personalize and invest in the philosophy as it relates to their individual practice. Its content focuses on the nursing department's vision and direction, actualization of the collaborative governance model, and the sharing of experiences from the department's rich history and current practice that support patient advocacy.

The Personal Mastery Program

Personal Mastery—The Nurse as a Person, Colleague, and Integrator of Care is a three-day retreat in which nurses can come together to reflect on the art of nursing. They experience caring, healing of self and others, strengthening relationships, learning as a lifelong endeavor, and the joy and value of humor and lightheartedness in the work setting. Each nurse defines strategies to move his or her personal vision into practice.

On the first day of the retreat, participants focus on understanding themselves by identifying their personal visions and preferred work and learning styles; on exploring how to achieve a healthy balance of mind, body, and spirit; and on discussing how these factors influence their work with others. On the second day, the retreat centers on understanding others and the nursing profession, with participants exploring caring and curing behaviors from a nursing and a patient perspective. Patients also participate, sharing stories of what it was like to be patients and describing the systems and care they experienced. On the final day of the retreat, nurses concentrate on understanding the shared vision of the department, comparing their vision of professional practice to the shared vision of nursing practice at Abbott Northwestern. There is an emphasis on change mastery and developing a hardiness for change from a secure professional base.

In essence, personal mastery offers nurses protected time in a restful setting to reflect on the meaning of their practice through guided experiences. Participants are from all practice areas; and each group develops a charter for caring and has a six-month reunion.

Establishment of the Center for Professional and Clinical Development

In view of the changing health care environment and the need to focus on added value to patient care and practice, the role of the clinical education specialist at Abbott Northwestern was redefined. As a result, the Nursing Education Department became the Center for Professional and Clinical Development (the center), with a more clearly defined focus and an emphasis on reducing costs and improving clinical and professional practice.

The center provides education leadership and consultation for individuals, nursing units, and groups through three service areas:

1. *Professional development:* Several programs for professional development have been established. In addition to the Advocacy through Caring and Personal Mastery programs described earlier, these include Leadership Seminar—The Staff Nurse as Leader; Preceptor Development—Teacher and Coach; Coaching and Mentoring—A Guide for Nurse Leaders; Collaboration—Key to Quality and Innovation; and Development Opportunities—Organizational Leadership.
2. *Clinical development:* Orientation, competency-based practice, in-services, and mandatory education requirements.
3. *Learning services:* Conferences, recognition programs, outreach, writing and publishing, career guidance, academic alliances, individual consultation, and practice support.

The center is designed around learning, with emphasis on the professional accountability of each nurse to enhance patient care through active participation in the process of learning and its application to practice.

Emphasis on the application of learning at the point of care is based on this question: What are the clinical and professional skills and knowledge required to support patients/families through times of crisis or trauma associated with illness? Nurses' work also focuses on this question: What is required to maximize the patient's ability to return home with the optimal level of health and well-being?

As part of the department's philosophy, educators are understood to be enablers of learning rather than content experts. As such, they create

106

an environment that provides a safe place for people to express diversity and increase understanding.

Practices of Exemplary Leaders

Kouzes's and Posner's work on practices of exemplary leaders is a useful framework for nurse leaders/consultants as they articulate their scope of practice and implement their role.[10] The practices of exemplary leaders are described as challenging the process, inspiring a shared vision, enabling others to act, modeling the way, and encouraging the heart. This has served to facilitate the developmental strategies for nurse leaders/consultants to increase their capacity to fulfill their roles.

A Comprehensive Curriculum for Quality Improvement

The consulting and development department created quality education /development building blocks to further the work of quality within nursing and to integrate nursing into the total quality environment. (See figure 5.) Programs and workshops were included to create competencies in self-knowledge, relationship versatility, cultural knowledge, process involvement, customer-focused work, team leadership, productive meetings, organizational alignment, systemic thinking, management skills, collaborative organizational design, and clinical process improvement.

Improved Labor–Management Relationships Based on a Professional Vision

Intentional relationship building occurred between the hospital and the Minnesota Nurses Association, the union representing staff nurses at Abbott Northwestern Hospital, to ensure the union had the respect and legitimacy it required to legally represent the nurses. Great care regarding inclusion, exploring common interests, and generating options to resolve issues, as well as a principle of "no surprises," guided the efforts. The search to identify common interests and engage in discussions of separate interests required practice and greater skill development. This effort resulted in greater creativity and flexibility with regard to options than had been possible previously, as well as greater understanding by management of union issues and greater appreciation by the union of management issues, interests, and requirements.

Implementation of the Clinical Practice Model

The clinical practice model is a system that supports the effective, individualized delivery of nursing care to patients based on their holistic care requirements and the art and science of professional nursing practice. (See figure 6

107

Figure 5. Quality Education/Development Building Blocks

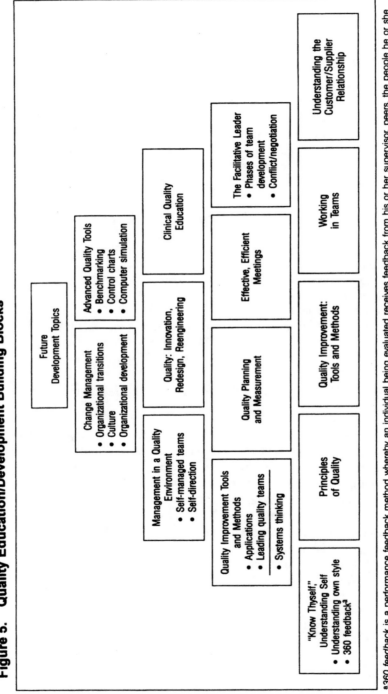

[a] 360 feedback is a performance feedback method whereby an individual being evaluated receives feedback from his or her supervisor, peers, the people he or she supervises, and key customers.

Source: Used with permission of Abbott Northwestern Hospital. Minneapolis.

Figure 6.   Professional Practice Model

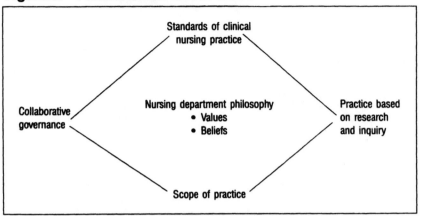

Source: Used with permission of Abbott Northwestern Hospital, Minneapolis.

Its goal is to define consistency in practice, ensure appropriateness of care, and decrease costs of care through increased efficiency, focus, and comprehensiveness. The model:

- Provides a framework for addressing the appropriateness, efficiency, and effectiveness of practice; aligns all of the activities in the department in a way that makes sense and strengthens nursing care delivery
- Reflects nursing department philosophy and standards
- Ties nursing to the work of the overall hospital and the managed care environment in which it exists
- Creates greater avenues for interdisciplinary, patient-focused collaboration

Implementation of a clinical practice model began when more than 80 nurses attended presentations on three professional practice models under consideration. The model that was selected originated from the Clinical Practice Model Resource Center in Grand Rapids, Michigan, with Bonnie Wesorick, founder and president. Implementation is expected to take 18 to 36 months. Of great value is that the model provides a common language and common performance standards and measurements—essential elements in creating a culture of high-quality practice.

Programs Designed to Respond to the Business Environment

Within the context of improved relations and skill enhancement, Abbott Northwestern launched a number of specific programs intended to respond to the new business environment. These included:

109

- A clinical nurse specialist group practice
- Nurse-to-nurse consultation
- The Hometown Nurse program
- Clinical nursing research

Clinical Nurse Specialist Group Practice

A multispecialty clinical nurse specialist (CNS) group practice was established to ensure coordination of patient care with maximum attention to quality and value. CNS group practice members partner with physician colleagues and collaborate with primary nurses, quality management specialists, and other members of the health care team to improve patient outcomes. They are population-based rather than unit- or program-based resources.

Previously, CNSs had been decentralized, reporting to divisional directors of nursing. There was a high variability in role implementation, and much of the role was focused toward support of projects, policies, and procedures. Now, CNSs provide nursing case management for high-risk patients, provide consultation and education on clinical issues of care, expand the use and development of clinical pathways for patient populations, and participate in interdisciplinary quality activities that address patient care issues.

Nurse-to-Nurse Consultation

Nurse-to-nurse consultation comprises a range of programs, products, and services designed to encourage nurses to share their expertise on clinical decision making and care delivery and to develop professional collaborative relationships to improve patient care. The program's goals are to create relationships and partnerships with nurses in rural communities, provide informational links for better continuity and patient-centered care, provide clinical and educational consultative services, and coordinate services at Abbott Northwestern for better access and use of resources. Program projects include an ongoing mechanism for monitoring calls to referring units, improvements in continuity of care on transfer and discharge, and creation of the *Nurse-to-Nurse Consultation Directory,* which includes an overview of 25 areas of nursing expertise, a listing of the nursing consultation services available in those areas, and the individuals available for consultation.

The Hometown Nurse Program

The Hometown Nurse program was created to promote sponsorship, a personalized environment, and continuity-of-care strategies for referral populations coming from regional settings to a hospital located in an urban environment. It helps out-of-state patients and their families feel more comfortable about being hospitalized far from home by linking them with nurses from the same hometown or region who can act as sponsors to help them navigate the intricacies of hospital care and the urban environment. In addition, the program links primary and tertiary care and builds relationships with patients, families, and health care professionals in both the hospital and the community. It recognizes the essential role of community care to patient outcomes. Program objectives are to create nurse partnerships among health care providers, to provide informational links for increased continuity and patient-centered care, and to create a hometown feel for patients hospitalized at Abbott Northwestern.

The Hometown Nurse program is an extension of Abbott Northwestern's care coordination, with 32 percent of the hospital's patient base being referred to Minneapolis from regional areas. It is now available to patients from 23 communities.

Clinical Nursing Research

The ultimate purpose of clinical nursing research at Abbott Northwestern Hospital is to promote scientific strategies to improve patient care. This represents a collaborative undertaking to bring nurse clinicians and scientists together at the patient bedside so that the practicing nurse can become a discriminate consumer of nursing research, use research findings in practice, and learn processes of clinical inquiry. This effort results in a data-based approach to nursing practice. A sense of inquiry, excitement, and intellectual challenge is present among the many nurses who participate directly or indirectly in these initiatives.

Nursing research ensures the attainment of new knowledge; creates a progressive, humanistic learning atmosphere; and values professional nursing practice. It helps nurses focus as one collaborative entity on the priority of nursing—patient care.

One successful nursing research project involved standardizing the approach to care for pressure ulcer patients, a vulnerable patient population. This standardization improved outcomes and reduced costs. The project resulted in savings of $50,000 over two months across seven patient care units. Ultimately, the project could save as much as $700,000 a year if implemented throughout the hospital.

Epicenters of Change

Throughout the past four years, within these overall departmental changes, patient care redesign has been occurring, supported in part by a grant from the Robert Wood Johnson Foundation/Pew Charitable Trusts called Strengthening Hospital Nursing: A Program to Improve Patient Care. In an environment of market-responsive change, it is a challenge to identify which change is the result of which stimulus. The grant work opened Abbott Northwestern's thinking to the larger community, reinforced partnerships with its customers, and was a catalyst to learning. The integration of quality, grant, strategic, and financial initiatives supported development of a more disciplined, results-oriented, customer-driven nursing department.

The grant sponsored three epicenters of change. These included:

1. Redesign of the rehabilitative care process
2. Redesign of the critical care process
3. Redesign of the cardiovascular care process

The methodology for work redesign was built on the foundation of collaborative governance, the Advocacy through Caring program, personal mastery, and the quality curriculum. The model used is an adaptation from the industrial reengineering work of Michael Hammer and the system-learning organization work of Peter Senge and Innovation Associates. (See figure 7.)

Nurses were among the process owners of these large system changes and worked with a design team to create the vision, design, and pilot for change. Targets were established, and results are being measured in the areas of:

- Improved clinical outcomes
- Increased patient/family satisfaction
- More meaningful work
- Increased efficiency of systems (for example, process simplification, reduced cycle times, and so on)
- Reduced costs

Figure 8 shows a model of the redesign team's organization.

Patients and payers were included on the design team as co-creators of change. The preliminary results are promising. Migrating from these epicenters are the extensions of innovation and CQI initiatives.

Innovations in infrastructure to support learning and change include personal mastery, team skills, curricula in CQI tools and methods, market/customer data feedback, and process owners and leaders.

Conclusion

Disciplines borrowed from business and industry, which were applied with full recognition of the mission, roles, and services of health care, have improved Abbott Northwestern's nursing department's focus and performance and have produced results. The key has been first "personalizing"

112

Figure 7. Innovation for Team Learning

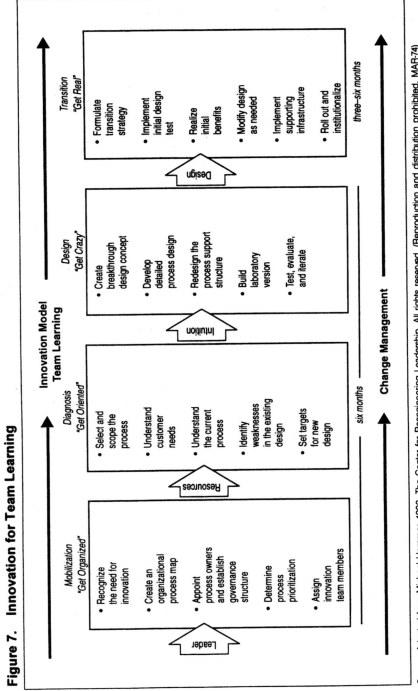

Innovation Model
Team Learning

Mobilization
"Get Organized"

- Recognize the need for innovation
- Create an organizational process map
- Appoint process owners and establish governance structure
- Determine process prioritization
- Assign innovation team members

Diagnosis
"Get Oriented"

- Select and scope the process
- Understand customer needs
- Understand the current process
- Identify weaknesses in the existing design
- Set targets for new design

Design
"Get Crazy"

- Create breakthrough design concept
- Develop detailed process design
- Redesign the process support structure
- Build laboratory version
- Test, evaluate, and iterate

Transition
"Get Real"

- Formulate transition strategy
- Implement initial design test
- Realize initial benefits
- Modify design as needed
- Implement supporting infrastructure
- Roll out and institutionalize

Leader → Resources → Intuition → Design

six months   *three–six months*

Change Management

Source: Adapted from Michael Hammer, 1992, The Center for Reengineering Leadership. All rights reserved. (Reproduction and distribution prohibited. MAR-74)

113

Figure 8. Organizational Structure of the Nursing Department's Redesign Team

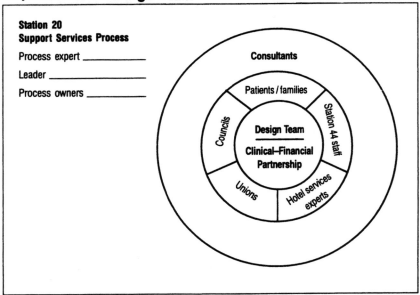

Source: Used with permission of Abbott Northwestern Hospital, Minneapolis.

the technologies and then applying them consistently. Identifying customer requirements, performance measures, and key organizational processes provided focus to the department's work. The capacity of the organization to improve and innovate was increased through development of internal consultants and experts who could lead personal mastery and change; teach and model the theory, tools, and methods of quality and reengineering; and create a culture of learning. Use of a patient-centered philosophy and vision grounded the nursing department in its purpose. Focus on the patient, involvement of stakeholders, and a grassroots approach to change have helped attenuate the fear often expressed in health care that use of business and industrial engineering practice in care delivery will result in a mechanistic, reductionistic, linear, by-the-numbers assembly-line environment for practice and will exclude the care provider's personal relationship with patients. However, the business discipline, when responding to customer/stakeholder requirements, can be liberating by providing focus and the technologies to realize that:

Patients are the reason we exist.
People are the reason we excel.
Systems support the work.

Appendix. Highlights of Requirements for Practice in the New Business Environment

Effects of managed competition on patient care delivery:

- Increased emphasis is placed on primary care, prevention, and community health improvement.
- The hospital is not the center of health care.
- Enrollees in a health plan, not the number of procedures or beds occupied, are a measure of success.
- Hospitals are a cost center; everything must add value.
- Data are a precious resource; they are measured and published.
- Systems and strategies for continuous care are needed more than ever.
- Service excellence is a competitive advantage that can be used to increase customer loyalty and market share.
- Customer loyalty facilitates long-term relationships, which create opportunities for health improvement.
- Efficiency, system improvement, and reduced costs of care are imperative.
- Providers have to redefine their roles and measures of success.
- Quantum-leap thinking is required.
- A moral compass considering philosophy, values, and beliefs is needed to guide decision making.

Requirements for successful practice/care delivery:

- Data-based practice, with continued scrutiny of variance to improve cost and outcome.
- Clarity of professional roles/responsibilities relating to effective and appropriate delegation and coordination.
- Team collaboration skills.
- Ability to learn and innovate.
- Facile, flexible organizational structure; no stovepipes or territories. The structure is based on customer requirements and key processes.
- Quality as a way of life. CQI skills are needed throughout the organization.
- Courage and intelligent risk taking.
- Excellent "customer-listening" skills and responsiveness to customer requirements.

Helpful organizational strategies:

- Develop customer-listening skills and methods.
- Understand clearly articulated, as well as latent, customer requirements.
- Identify, focus, and improve key processes.

- Establish group practices.
- Develop communities of care.
- Organize a focused managed care structure.
- Emphasize outreach and bridging strategies to communities.
- Establish innovation as an organizational focus.
- Develop information systems.
- Ensure that employee development efforts include strategies to increase employees' capacities to learn, change, and be flexible and versatile in their contributions.
- Understand and embrace diversity.

Characteristics of the effective nurse:

- Vision
- Clinical competence
- Hardiness for change
- Patient focused
- Versatile and flexible
- Grounded in quality principles and skills
- Communicator/collaborator
- Professional versus task focused
- Confidence in scope of practice

Educational strategies:

- Personal mastery
- Team learning
- Systems thinking
- Change theory
- CQI
- Delegation and collaboration
- Diversity

References

1. Slack, R. Interview by author. Abbott Northwestern Hospital, Minneapolis, 1994.

2. Goldsmith, J. C. The illusive logic of integration. *Healthcare Forum Journal* 37(5):26–31, Sept./Oct. 1994.

3. Goldsmith.

4. Creech, B. *The Five Pillars of TQM.* New York City: Truman Talley Books/Dutton, 1994, p. 201.

5. Miller, E. H., Perkins, D., Waggoner, D., Morath, J., and Miller, T. *Patient Care Delivery Model*. Minneapolis: Abbott Northwestern Hospital, 1994.

6. Oldencamp, M., and Carse, C. Blueprint for clinical and financial information. Working document presented at VHA CFIS User Meeting, Orlando, Nov. 14, 1994.

7. Gerteis, M. *Through the Patient's Eyes*. San Francisco: Jossey-Bass, 1993.

8. Peck, M. S. Community by choice, not chance. Presentation, The Master's Forum, Minneapolis, Apr. 8, 1992.

9. Senge, P. M. Transforming the practice of management. *Human Resource Development Quarterly* 4(1):5–32, Spring 1993.

10. Kouzes, J. M., and Posner, B. Z. *The Leadership Challenge: How to Get Extraordinary Things Done in Organizations*. San Francisco: Jossey-Bass, 1990.

SECTION FOUR

From Case Management to Medical Care Management

Policy Challenges

From Case Management
to Medical Care Management

Implications for Nursing Education

Barry R. Greene
Debra L. Kelsey

This chapter examines the traditional role of the registered nurse as case manager and explores how that role will change in the context of the managed systems of care outlined in Chapter One and described in greater depth in Chapter Four. As management of medical services becomes increasingly important, these systems will demand that some professionals exercise leadership in this area. Nursing professionals already have a significant amount of training and experience in case management and could be directed to expand their skill base to encompass the larger role of care manager needed by the new health systems. The chapter closes with suggestions on how the gap between RNs' current skills and those required for medical care management can be filled. The authors conclude that improving an RN's skills in analyzing and conducting health services research will be essential to narrowing this gap.

T he dramatic changes in the health care industry described in Chapter One and throughout this book are creating intense pressure to reduce costs, maintain revenues, and improve quality. These pressures are increasingly compelling health care providers to accept more accountability for lowering costs and improving quality. This emphasis has led to more active involvement on the part of health professionals in constructing measurement mechanisms that can demonstrate accountability and capacity to meet consumer needs. Figure 1 depicts the activities and processes of shared accountability. These activities involve learning and applying the tools of systems analysis and quality management. They also encompass new ways of thinking about the measurement of health care processes and inputs.

Establishing a clinically integrated health care system has become a predominant strategy for improving accountability. At the core of this strategy, care management programs provide for continuity of care across the continuum of services and clinical settings. Care management encompasses planning, assessment, and

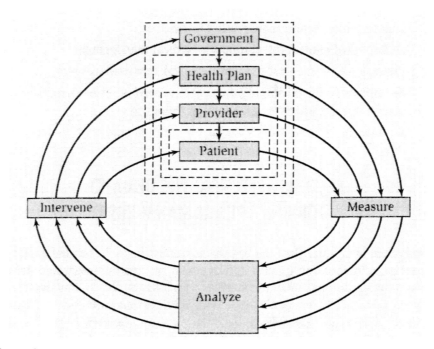

Figure 1   Medical Management and Shared Accountabilities Model.

Source: Strategic Consulting Services, 1995.

coordination of health services for the population managed by a delivery system. Some care management activities focus on individual patients, whereas others focus on the broad needs of the entire population a system serves.

In nearly every region of the country, the move toward clinical integration is changing the roles and responsibilities of health care professionals and the way they practice. RNs are becoming increasingly important in the delivery and management of care within integrated systems, because nursing traditionally has emphasized nurturing, generative, and holistic practices (American Nurses Association, 1981). Understanding and identifying the factors of successful clinical integration is important for RNs, who will be positioned to contribute to and take on leadership roles in the design, development, and evaluation of clinical processes. However, most nursing education programs have not traditionally focused on the concepts and clinical management skills required in the integrated system environment, especially those skills required to measure and evaluate the relation between cost and quality. Nursing education must adapt to this new and changing situation.

This chapter provides a review and analysis of the changing demand for RNs as care managers. Specifically, it addresses the following:

- Industry priorities and their driving forces
- The impact of clinical integration on medical management
- Nursing's role in medical management and care management
- The imperative for revamping nursing education to provide nurses with the new skills required for care management roles
- Retooling the nursing workforce for the care management model

FACTORS AFFECTING THE DEMAND
FOR RNS AS CARE MANAGERS

As first noted in Chapter One, the health care industry has responded to demand for cost containment and quality improvement by creating integrated delivery systems. Integration has been depicted as a philosophy that unites the mission and goals of health care organizations with services and providers, particularly the health professions (Lewicki, Miller, Whitman, and Coulter, 1995). Although integrated delivery systems are defined in a variety of ways, they may generally be thought of as organizations that, through ownership or contractual arrangements, provide a full spectrum of health care services and often also include health insurance functions. To achieve coordination, the delivery system is required to deliver care and manage illness in a comprehensive fashion, with an emphasis on physical, social, psychological, and spiritual health.

Ultimately, the overarching goal of integrated delivery systems is the integration of a continuum of clinical services, which, according to experts, increases system performance. Successful clinical integration is often measured by using indicators of failed integration such as duplicate tests and procedures, medication errors, decreased patient satisfaction, and so forth. Experts debate the relationships among indicators of lack of clinical integration, but three factors consistently emerge as critical success: physician leadership, efficient and timely information systems, and alignment of system incentives.

As managed care organizations have evolved, they have further defined clinical integration in the manner depicted in Table 1. The table illustrates the dramatic contrast between fee-for-service and managed care environments. Wheras dis-integration was the norm in the former system, integration is fundamental to the latter.

In addition, insurers and providers have sought to identify their competitive advantage in the form of core competencies (that is, a critical set of skills, knowledge, abilities, traits, and motivations that will be distinguishable and competitive in the marketplace) that address issues of cost containment, efficiency, and qual-

Table 1 Evolution of Clinical Integration

From	To
1. Managing inpatient care	1. Managing care across the system, regardless of site
2. Using prospective/retrospective cost control mechanism	2. Relying on real-time patient management systems
3. Single, clinician care management	3. Multidisciplinary team care management
4. Disintegrated system	4. Clinical congruence

ity. Recent research (Strategic Consulting Services, 1995) has identified six core managed care competencies: managing population health (medical management), bearing financial risk, building and maintaining partnerships, coordinating administrative functions, establishing and managing new and distinct cultures, and building powerful information linkages or infrastructure.

Population Health Management

The cornerstone and most challenging of these competencies is often the development of superior population health management, which in its broadest sense requires accountability and management of the health of an entire community, regardless of system membership or insurance status. Population health management requires managing not only medical care but also health promotion and disease prevention. To date, very few delivery systems or managed care entities have stepped up to the challenge of truly managing, or integrating, all factors that affect the health of an entire population (Strategic Consulting Services, 1995). However, many are implementing strategies for managing medical services.

Effective Medical Management and Clinical Integration

In this era of measurement of performance and value, the demand for results is increasingly paramount. Integrated systems, provider groups, and managed care organizations must design effective medical management programs that accomplish the goals of clinical integration and provide tangible evidence of effectiveness. Thus, the greatest challenge is to link medical management program(s) to the organization's bottom line. Those who support medical management contend that it is the most essential factor in achieving long-term business goals. However, historically, CEOs and company board members have been skeptical and slow to buy in.

Managerial leaders are most receptive when medical management's cost containment features are emphasized. Medical management addresses the 87 percent of the health care dollar that is spent on the provision and purchase of medical services (physician services, hospital care, home health, ambulatory care, prescription drugs, and other ancillary services and providers). To effectively reduce health care spending, ensure financial viability, and maintain competitive positioning, health care organizations must focus on controlling these medical costs.

Medical management programs also allow health care organizations to price competitively due to efficiency gains (for example, by directing resources to appropriate levels of care and coordination). These programs also provide avenues to focus on factors other than price (for example, quality and access). This second point is critical for differentiating a company from its competitors and maintaining satisfied customers (Strategic Consulting Services, 1995).

Figure 2 displays **major approaches to medical management, indicating** the frequency with which they are utilized by integrated delivery systems. Leading integrated delivery systems tend to rely most frequently on practice guidelines or clinical pathways in their current developmental efforts (Strategic Consulting Services, 1995). These guidelines are then used in a variety of ways, most frequently as a foundation for care management, disease management, and outcomes management programs (*Medical Group Practice Digest*, 1995).

Effective medical management and case management programs usually target one or more of the small number of diseases responsible for the majority of medical costs for the population managed by an integrated delivery system. Ac-

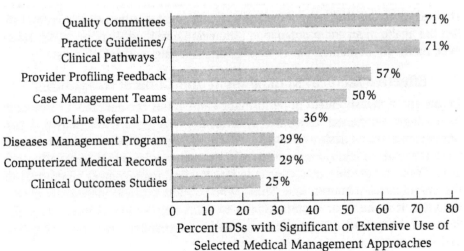

Percent IDSs with Significant or Extensive Use of Selected Medical Management Approaches

Figure 2. Medical Management Approaches

Source: Strategic Consulting Services, 1995

123

cording to Strategic Consulting Services (1995), the most expensive medical services in the United States involve treatment of cardiovascular diseases, childbirth complications, low back pain, breast cancer, asthma, and diabetes complications.

Evidence of the effectiveness of these programs is emerging. Those with tangible, published results include case management, disease management, traditional utilization management, demand management, and selected wellness and prevention programs (Strategic Consulting Services, 1995). For example, the results of a recent Health Insurance Association of America survey indicate that insurance carriers who had invested in disability and medical rehabilitation case management programs had a thirty-to-one savings on their investment, amounting to over $50 million between 1991 and 1993. There are many other examples of such savings (Schwartz, 1996, p. 6). Moreover, research has found that the degree to which integrated systems implement strong medical management approaches indicates the systems' relative potential for enhancing value in clinical care delivery.

Nursing's Role in Medical Management

Medical management is an increasingly critical element of health services administrators' efforts to plan, organize, coordinate, finance, evaluate, and deliver care because medical management directly addresses the cost and quality of services delivered. The increased emphasis on medical management represents a great opportunity for RNs, but unfortunately one for which many of them are ill prepared.

Shortell, Gillies, and Anderson (1994) predict that within the next five to ten years nursing will likely join the dominant coalition in health services management, which for the past thirty years consisted of governing board, management, and medical staff. Shortell believes that as a professional group RNs play critical roles throughout the health care delivery system because they are typically the primary resource coordinators who are most closely linked to the critical financial and clinical data.

Nursing has historically been a critical component in setting goals and fulfilling objectives for patient care in hospitals (Schulz and Johnson, 1990). Through the 1960s, 1970s, and into the 1980s, nursing adapted to the increasing advances in technology, changing environments, and expanding scope of hospital services. As nursing expanded its degree of specialization, clinical nurse specialists, nurse clinicians, and nurse practitioners were recognized for their advanced clinical competencies and given leadership roles for newly established nursing teams.

With the advent of Medicare's prospective payment system in the mid-1980s, nurses became a critical resource to hospitals, which began to scrutinize utilization, cost, and medical necessity issues. Faced with similar pressures to contain costs, insurance companies began employing nurses to conduct utilization management, claims review, and medical record reviews, as well as to perform traditional case management functions (Kellogg Foundation, 1990). "Nurses' vast experience as first-line unit-level managers enables them to provide valuable consultation to health care organizations as they struggle to address cost and quality concerns" (Schulz and Johnson, 1990).

Today, managed care organizations and integrated systems are hiring RNs to perform in a variety of critical roles. These include managers of quality improvement strategies, evaluators of treatment, and developers of protocols, disease management programs, outcomes management programs, and care management programs (Strategic Consulting Services, 1995; Kellogg Foundation, 1990). Nursing's roles in integrated health systems also include conducting clinical research, involvement in developing clinical information systems, leading physicians in the development of clinical pathways, and other leadership roles. Evolution in the roles of nurses allows for technical nursing (cure and care services) to advance both within and outside the hospital setting but, most importantly, for professional nursing to take on greater decision-making, leadership, and executive functions (Schulz and Johnson, 1990). RNs also continue to expand their roles in health services administration. The scope and role of nursing has continued to grow outside the hospital setting, with RNs taking leadership roles in developing hospital-based home health and hospice services, as well as wellness centers (Kellogg Foundation, 1990).

A VHA Inc. and American Organization of Nursing Executives study reported in July 1996 that nursing executives are "at the heart" of the organizational redesign currently taking place in health care (Gelinas and Manthey, 1996). The survey of two thousand nursing executives was developed to study the evolving roles of nurse leaders. The study examined the changes taking place nationwide in the health care delivery system over the last few years. Of the nursing leaders surveyed, 80 percent have seen their roles and authority expand. In addition, 85 percent worked in hospitals that were currently in the midst of a redesign; nearly 60 percent said they made or make redesign decisions jointly with the CEO. The most dramatic growth in nurse executive responsibility has occurred in respiratory therapy, social services, and pharmacy. Nearly 30 percent of the nurse executives surveyed said that pharmacy services now report to them.

The survey also found that nurses are being asked to acquire additional clinical skills so they can work in more than one area and to assume more responsibility for managing patient care. These changes are paralleled by changes in the use of unlicensed assistive personnel. Half the nurses indicated restructuring has resulted in increased use of multiskilled, unlicensed personnel, especially in the phlebotomy, electrocardiogram administration, and respiratory therapy fields (Gelinas and Manthey, 1996).

From Case Managers to Care Managers

Two of the most important roles of nurses in emerging delivery systems are as case managers and care managers. Case management first appeared in the public health arena to provide coordination of community services, with nurses managing their work by caseloads (Lewicki, Miller, Whitman, and Coulter, 1995). Along a similar timeline, case management became a key function of health insurance companies, where nurses monitor and influence medical care provided to patients, typically those with a high-cost illness or disorder (Strategic Consulting Services, 1995).

The goals of case management, both historically and today, have focused on coordination, cost containment, quality of care, and collaboration. As case managers, nurses follow a process similar to physician decision making by assessing needs, developing diagnoses, planning interventions, implementing interventions, and evaluating outcomes. Nurse case managers essentially plan health care services and integrate them across the health care delivery continuum (Horn and Hopkins, 1994). The benefits of such programs are becoming increasingly important in today's environment.

Care management extends the functions and philosophies of case management (managing individual cases) to an entire population. Successful care management requires a team approach. Typically, care management teams include nurses, physicians, physician extenders, medical assistants, ancillary providers, nutritionists, psychotherapists, and other alternative care givers (Capko and Sage, 1995). Additionally, care management teams define their target population either by disease or by need (for example, prevention and education).

Tools typically used in care teams include clinical pathways, disease management programs, and benchmarking data and analyses. Often care management encompasses collecting and coordinating information from physicians, nurses, ancillary providers, managed care organizations, and the patients themselves (Strategic Consulting Services, 1995). Care management often cuts across a multitude of settings, from preventive care to home care, rehabilitation, and community care, creating an ideal mechanism for managing services and outcomes within integrated systems of care (Lewicki, Miller, Whitman, and Coulter, 1995).

Case management and care management are being implemented in hospitals to facilitate better management of care delivery and associated costs. Nursing is positioned and being called upon to lead care management teams and case management programs. As integrated systems evolve, further development of nurses' case and care management skills will be critical to success. Currently, advanced degrees (either master's or practitioner level) tend to be required by integrated systems where specialty service (high risk or chronic disease) populations are targeted, such as in oncology or obstetrics (Strategic Consulting Services, 1995). The roles for associate, baccalaureate, and master's prepared nurses will become more distinct as nurses in care and case management positions take on greater accountability for the delivery systems' performance.

CHANGING NURSING EDUCATION

What does the emergence of medical management mean for nursing education? There is clearly a serious need in the health services field for close examination of the cost-quality relationship as a routine part of system activities. Health professions education is not preparing health professionals to undertake these activities despite strong market demand for them.

Reexamining Core and Collateral Knowledge Areas

Health administrators and physicians are educated to examine either the cost *or* the quality dimension, respectively, rather than the relation between the two. Although cost-quality analysis should not be the exclusive domain of one profession, nursing is positioned to respond directly to the need to analyze the cost-quality relationship. The challenge is for nursing education to integrate cost and quality measurement techniques into the curriculum at all degree levels.

Advocating the inclusion of cost-quality knowledge development in the nursing educational system is not to say that health care is a commodity. Clearly, patients may be mistreated with an overemphasis on cost management. However, an informed analysis of the two variables simultaneously represents a responsible approach to meeting the public's needs in a managed care environment.

The Pew Health Professions Commission's report *Critical Challenges: Revitalizing the Health Professions for the Twenty-First Century* (1995) recommends a number of curricular reforms to better prepare health professionals for practice in the emerging system. Two recommendations are particularly relevant to expanding the scope and depth of the nursing curriculum to include cost-quality analysis.

The first recommendation: "All health professional schools must enlarge the scientific bases of their education programs to include the psychosocial behavioral sciences and population and health management sciences in an evidence based approach to the clinical work" (p. 22). Health professions education must encompass behavioral and social science research methods and the measurement techniques that can be applied in program evaluation and the analysis of the health behavior of specific populations.

The second recommendation: "The next generation of professionals must be prepared to practice in settings that are more intensively managed and integrated" (p. 22). RNs and other health professionals will be expected to apply the techniques of cost-quality analysis as members of interdisciplinary teams.

These teams will analyze data from integrated management and clinical information systems, develop appropriate responses, and then analyze the data again to determine whether outcome targets have been met. A sound understanding of this context is as critical to effective care management as knowledge of cost-quality analysis techniques.

Process Identification and Quality Management. Much of this interdisciplinary activity involves process identification. Process identification is based on the simple notion that all activities in the health services system can be conceived of as steps in a process of converting inputs to outputs (James, 1989). The documentation and specification of processes in health care and medical management are largely team activities. In both health services and medical management the first step in knowledge improvement is documentation and specification of measurable processes that can be controlled and managed. Process identification emphasizes control of variation and can be implemented successfully only as a recurring set of continuous efforts toward quality improvement. Quality improvement is a rapidly developing area in the health services field. This approach is not new, but typically it is underemphasized in most traditional health professions educational programs.

The techniques and functions that support process identification and quality improvement involve assessment, project management, measurement, benchmarking, and strategic analysis. The many tools of process identification and quality management include flowcharting, cause-effect diagramming, cost-benefit analysis, and relationship charting. Preparation in statistical processes and quality control analysis has a special meaning and importance in applications to health services.

Medical management is rapidly becoming a more precise knowledge area within the broader framework of health services administration. It requires knowing more about service program objectives and acquiring the tools and language for program evaluation. Medical management and associated process identification and quality improvement techniques should be a component of core knowledge in the preparation of nurses, at least at the advanced practice level.

Typically, nursing administration curriculum is offered as a graduate-level elective taught exclusively by nursing school faculty. This approach is no longer adequate. It is simply not enough to know on an elective basis a little about the administrative principles within the narrow field of nursing services. Nurses and nursing education can and should contribute more directly to an improved accounting of the quality of care and quality of the overall system.

Professional Education: Integrating Theory and Practice. The implications of these recommendations for nursing education merit specific discussion within the broader context of professional education. A professionally oriented academic program is considered strong to the degree that it effectively integrates theory and practice. The tasks of an academic program are teaching, professional service, and research. These academic tasks contribute to the identity, stability, and ultimately to the legitimization of the profession. If educators do not perform these academic tasks well the professional knowledge base and its legitimization are at stake (Abbott, 1991).

At present, academic nursing does not contribute significantly to the scope and depth of the knowledge relating to the cost-quality complexities involved in the direct provision of nursing care. Cost-quality analysis is a neglected area in the educational development of the professional nurse and too often neglected as well in the academic interests and research capabilities of nursing faculty. These are unmet responsibilities that, if addressed in nursing education curricula, could significantly improve the performance of practicing nurse professionals.

Scope and Depth of Academic Content: The Integrated Technology Curriculum. A curriculum may be defined simply as a series of structured learning sequences. That being the case, in nursing it may be instructive to think in terms of the descriptive scope of curriculum content that cuts horizontally across the disciplines such as the social and behavioral sciences while depth constitutes a vertical axis with advanced clinical study in particular specialties as its apex. One expects to find more descriptive content at the beginning levels of professional education. A curriculum builds by adding analytic depth as generic concepts are applied to phenomena within the domain of professional interest and responsibility. Nursing education must address both the scope and the depth of cost-quality phenomena. The traditional nursing curriculum not only lacks sufficient content in cost-quality analysis but also fails to progress from descriptive to more advanced and abstract analysis.

One way to examine this issue conceptually across all levels of nursing education is presented in the Integrated Technology curriculum, as illustrated in Figure 3. **This model illustrates the academic context for nursing education.** The model begins with the core knowledge areas of nursing theory and practice. Knowledge improvement analysis and tools and research methods should be added to the core knowledge areas. The collateral areas in this new model would be in epidemiology and biostatistics, medical management, and health services administration. The intended emphasis on the scope and depth of the core and collateral areas in advanced practice and graduate nursing makes the model important.

Direct patient care is the traditional clinical focus of nursing education and will not be elaborated on here. This focus extends up through advanced practice nursing. This academic content remains at the distinctive center of the nursing profession. However, at all levels nursing curricula should encompass more attention to the knowledge improvement techniques and tools, which are necessary

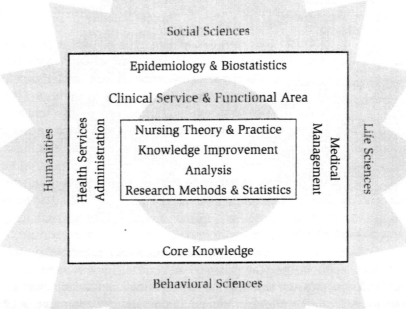

Figure 3. Integrated Technology Curriculum Model for Nursing

Source: Greene, 19

to understand the cost-quality relationship. These techniques and tools are listed **in Table 2.**

Better preparation in statistics and other research methods is especially critical. Managed care systems are much more data and information driven than the earlier institutional-based system. The nurse in the managed care environment needs an objective understanding of the content and flow of clinical and administrative work activity. Working within a context of practice guidelines, clinical pathways, and evidence-based systems requires an understanding of objective data collection and analysis. Basic concepts of validity, reliability, and so forth separate research-based standards from the criteria required to form consensus judgments. Nurse professionals need to understand and apply these concepts.

130

Table 2. Knowledge Improvement Techniques and Tools

• KI Techniques	• KI Tools
Quality Improvement	For Data Collection
Projects and Teams	Data Analysis
Models for Improvement	Process Stability
Tools for Process	Control Charts
Description	For Collaborative Work
Flowcharts	Composite techniques
Cause-effect diagrams	
Models for Process Design	• Measurement Techniques
Clinical paths	Clinical Outcomes
Models for Strategic Planning	Customer Perceptions of Quality
Customer Needs Analysis	Internal Process
Dimensions of quality	Performance
Focus groups and surveys	Financial Performance
	Benchmarking

Source: Adapted from Plsek, 1995

Basic research methods also can help the nurse professional describe and explain variation in practice. For example, understanding and controlling professional practice patterns is becoming increasingly important for health professionals of different types. Understanding the processes behind variation in practice patterns is one of the primary results of knowledge improvement analysis.

The Current Misalignment of Nursing Education

In the judgment of the authors of this chapter, nursing education at present does not effectively integrate knowledge improvement techniques and tools. This is the case across all of the degree areas and includes both the collateral and core areas recommended in the Integrated Technology model. The current levels of nursing education differentiate content based on clinical service knowledge areas (such as oncology or pediatrics) and functional areas such as nursing administration. This separation seems to diminish the development of analytic content in both the core curriculum and the collateral areas.

Nursing education curricula must be modified to place greater emphasis on analytic tools used to analyze cost-quality relationships. Understanding data collection and evaluative analysis is important at all levels of nursing education, although familiarity with research results or actually participating in research is probably not important below the baccalaureate or professional nurse level. Knowledge of the philosophy of science and the accumulation of scientific evidence also is obviously very important to comprehension of the evolution of practice guidelines as well as the establishment of evidence-based health outcomes. In addition, nurses need to know how the concepts and tools of program evaluation can be applied to process identification and quality management.

ANA Research Standards for Each Level of Nursing Education

Currently, the standards for education in research reflect the guidelines established by the American Nurses Association (ANA) Commission on Nursing Research in 1981. The commission developed standards for nursing education in research at four levels: associate, baccalaureate's, master's, and doctoral (American Nurses Association, 1981). These standards emphasize progression from consumer to scholar as an individual completes further education in nursing. The ANA commission recommended that associate and baccalaureate education focus on developing skills for consuming research, with master's and doctoral students obtaining the additional skills required to conduct research and develop theory. The standards suggest that nursing research should be primarily concerned with clinical nursing practice. However, the standards do not enumerate specific research concepts and techniques that students should acquire at each level of nursing education.

Although the ANA commission's guidelines do point to important areas of research training, the authors of this chapter think that research in nursing education should focus more on evaluative research concept skills that could be directly applied to knowledge development in the area of quality improvement and management in health services organizations. Specifically, research training should emphasize understanding of scientific methods of collecting and analyzing data in relation to practice. At the higher levels of nursing education, it should also stress integrating outside disciplinary approaches with nursing research.

In addition, the authors recommend a reevaluation of faculty competencies and the academic content of the nursing education curriculum. Nursing faculty and their academic programs need to be much more fully integrated into the broader academic community. The academic knowledge bases of all health professions are becoming increasingly interdisciplinary and cannot be advanced within the narrow limits of a professional knowledge perspective. Further, innovation in nursing education should encompass redesigning and cutting back on existing programs rather than simply adding new ones.

Matching Content with Education Level in Nursing

To ensure that RNs have the analytical tools they will need to thrive in the emerging health services environment, the authors recommend the following changes at each level of nursing education.

132

Associate. Associate programs should focus on professional knowledge. The descriptive aspects of nursing theory and clinical practice are best acquired and delivered at this level. Because the content is descriptive the knowledge is time bound. However, the wisdom that can accumulate through years of clinical observation should not be underestimated. The challenge is to provide a broad disciplinary conceptual base to permit valid clinical classifications for specific services and patient settings. Good clinical faculty and service settings are needed. The effective coordination of strong clinical experiences is important, yet takes nursing faculty away from the kinds of scholarly activities that are rewarded in university settings. For this reason, in associate-level programs these experiences might be better provided in new partnerships with health service systems. These systems certainly do not need to be academic health centers. In fact, educational needs may be better served in primary care settings.

Bachelor. It would seem that at this professional nurse level, the collateral and core content should be much more thoroughly examined than at present. This is where the opportunity exists to reexamine the entire four-year model to strike a better balance among the areas emphasized in the Integrated Technology model. The quality and legitimacy of academic knowledge in nursing can be strengthened if it is reconfigured in ways that build on the disciplinary scope and depth that exists on the campuses of research universities. Much experimental and demonstration work probably can be done in the health science centers of these universities, due to the availability of clinical sites and pressure to lower clinical services costs without jeopardizing quality. At the same time, new clinical partnerships are needed outside academic health centers to provide strong clinical education in primary and ambulatory care.

Advanced Practice. Understandably, associate and bachelor's degree programs are bound by college and university general education requirements and academic policies in general. Graduate and certificate programs are much less constrained. This is where the Integrated Technology model can pay off if the core and collateral areas are packaged not only in traditional degree programs, but also in certificate and nontraditional and executive program offerings.

The distinction drawn between a clinical service specialty and a functional area such as nursing administration should be reconsidered. If the core and collateral areas indicated in the Integrated Technology model can be developed, the nurse will be able to play a greater role than that of either a nursing administrator or a clinical specialist. Knowledge improvement capabilities can both contribute to the scientific base of the clinical specialist's performance and enhance the expertise of the nurse administrator.

Doctoral. The ability of nurses to gain disciplinary depth in teaching and research is an important step in the development of academic knowledge in nursing. The importance of the disciplinary method in academic programming deserves reemphasis. As the approach moves from the descriptive to the analytic and so should the rigor of nursing education. Knowledge development in the area of quality improvement and medical management content should be strongly emphasized in doctoral education programs, because doing so will strengthen the scientific base and provide analytic rigor to the course of study for both the faculty and students. The ultimate result will be a wider and deeper academic knowledge base, which in turn helps both the practice and the academic communities in which professionals serve.

Issues Surrounding Retraining
of the Existing Nursing Workforce

Given the changes occurring in the health care system, many nurses will need additional education and training. A short-term solution to this problem could be the education of professional nurses in critical skill components such as cost-benefit analysis, information systems, population health management, and continuous quality improvement. Additional education in these areas, which are not likely to be a part of any RN's academic preparation, would probably contribute directly to enhanced job performance. The scope, depth, and rigor of this skill development could be adapted for different nursing degree levels and positions and levels of education.

CONCLUSION

Policymakers, analysts, and participants in the health service system agree on the priority of improving the cost-effectiveness of health care services. Because nurses are patient oriented and have a wealth of experience in direct patient care, they are in a unique position to contribute to and lead analysis of both the cost and quality dimensions of health services. Nurses' effectiveness in cost-quality analysis will be determined by both their practical experience and professional education.

Nursing has already helped direct and integrate provider teams to best serve the patient. Nurses have the opportunity to lead the health professions to a higher level of academic integration, now that teams of providers and organizations must listen to consumers and be accountable for their professional performance. As professional domains continue to be reexamined in the light of the restructuring generated by the forces of managed care, higher levels of academic achievement and professional responsibility will be required. This will

134

entail taking some risk by opening up the profession, collaborating in academic circles, and cutting across professional boundaries. Moreover, this will mean viewing the emerging health care environment as an opportunity to expand nurses' roles rather than as a threat to the profession.

References

Abbott, A. *The Systems of Professions.* Chicago: University of Chicago Press, 1991.

American Nurses Association. *Guidelines for the Investigative Functions of Nurses.* Kansas City, Mo.: American Nurses Association, 1981.

Capko, J., and Sage, M. J. "Care Teams: A Practical Approach to Managed Care." *American Medical News,* 1995, *38*(44), 23.

Gelinas, L. S., and Manthey, M. *The Impact of Organizational Redesign on Nurse Executive Leadership,* Part II. Irving, Tex.: VHA, 1996.

Greene, B. R. "Trends, Issues, and Models in Health Services and Health Policy Programs in Business School Settings." In P. Leatt and B. R. Greene (eds.), "Accreditation in the Health Professions," *Journal of Health Administration Education,* Winter 1996.

Horn, S., and Hopkins, D. S. "Clinical Practice Improvement: A New Technology for Developing Cost-Effective Quality." In *Health Care,* Vol. 1. New York: Faulkner & Gray, 1994.

James, B. C. *Quality Management for Health Care Delivery—Quality Measurement and Management Project.* Chicago: Hospital Research and Educational Trust, 1989.

Kellogg Foundation. *Nursing's Vital Signs—Shaping the Profession for the 1990s.* Battle Creek, Mich.: W. K. Kellogg Foundation, 1990.

Lewicki, L. J., Miller, C. M., Whitman, G. R., and Coulter, S. J. "Nursing Case Management: Coordinating a Seamless Continuum of Care." In *Integrated Health Care Delivery Systems: A Guide to Successful Strategies for Hospital and Physician.* Washington, D.C.: Thompson, July 1995.

Medical Group Practice Digest. Kansas City, Mo.: Hoechst Marion Roussel, 1995.

Pew Health Professions Commission. *Critical Challenges: Revitalizing the Health Professions for the Twenty-First Century.* San Francisco: UCSF Center for the Health Professions, 1995.

Plsek, P. E. "Techniques for Managing Quality." *Hospital and Health Services Administration,* Spring 1995.

Schulz, R., and Johnson, A. *Management of Hospitals and Health Services: Strategic Issues and Performance.* (3rd ed.) St. Louis, Mo.: Mosby, 1990.

Schwartz, M. P. "Case Management Programs Show Solid Returns." *National Underwriter Property & Casualty-Risk Benefits Management,* 1996, *3,* 6.

Shortell, S. M., Gillies, R. R., and Anderson, D. A. "The New World of Managed Care: Creating Organized Delivery Systems. *Health Affairs,* Winter 1994, pp. 46–63.

Strategic Consulting Services. *Database.* Chicago: Strategic Consulting Services, 1995.

Policy Challenges

Joel Shalowitz

Joel Shalowitz is professor and director of the health services management program at the J. L. Kellogg Graduate School of Management, Northwestern University, and professor of medicine at Northwestern's medical school. He is the managing partner for a primary care group with more than twenty practitioners, and he practices internal medicine with the group. A Fellow of the American College of Physicians, he also serves as a board member for the Academy for Healthcare Organizations, Network for Healthcare Management and Research, and Alexian Brothers Medical Center.

As our society modifies traditional notions of health care cost, quality, access, and insurance yet retains an ideal of patient freedom of choice, conflicts are arising that require us to make critical decisions not only about how many resources we can consume but what trade-offs we can afford. These modifications are examined here, along with the challenges they present and the trade-offs and conflicts that arise from the U.S. public's wanting it all.

INSURANCE BENEFITS

The original purpose of insurance was to indemnify the policyholder against catastrophic risk. Such risk came from acute illnesses or injuries. In keeping with this notion, commercial insurance evolved from covering only hospital care (the most expensive item, as early as the 1930s) to covering physician services and then to paying for medical devices and approved pharmaceuticals. More recently a number of special interest groups have successfully lobbied state legislatures to mandate benefits that do not meet the definition of catastrophic illness. These benefits range from wigs for chemotherapy patients to infertility services. Further, they increase the cost of care for all. The health insurance question of most concern has therefore changed from *what* should be covered (apparently everything politically expedient) to *how much* insurance companies and individuals will pay.

In order to avoid the constraints of such mandatory benefits, many companies have taken advantage of their option under the Employee Retirement Income Security Act (ERISA) to design their own benefit packages for the workers they cover. Realistic policymakers understand that on the one hand, if we are to implement substantial health reform in this country, ERISA exemptions must be challenged; on the other hand, if these exemptions are modified or eliminated, many fear some businesses will eliminate health care coverage entirely.

Challenge. Reformulate health policy so that basic health insurance can include only those services and products necessary for prevention, treatment, and palliation of illness.

DEMOGRAPHICS

The fastest percentage growth in any age group is in people over eighty-five years old. Further, the first members of the baby boom generation became fifty in 1996. In considering these statistics, we often focus on the health needs of the increasing number of elderly. Equally important, however, is that there are proportionately fewer younger persons to pay for care for the elderly (particularly through the Medicare system) and to provide nonreimbursable caretaking services.

138

Challenge. Through more efficient use of current resources and targeted research, identify strategies that will prolong the functional life of the elderly. (Cost challenges are discussed later.)

VALUE

The nexus of cost and quality considerations is value. *Value* can be defined as the best quality one can obtain for a given price or as payment of the lowest price for a desired level of quality. In order to gauge whether we are getting value from our health care systems, we need to decide what it is we want to maximize. Our traditional focus has been on acute illness and disease care rather than health care. Early in this century we appropriately devoted resources to public health measures like infection control. When infectious diseases were no longer the chief cause of mortality in this country, resources were directed at and technology was developed to treat the ailments that succeeded infectious diseases as the leading causes of death—heart disease and cancers. Although no one would argue the wisdom of saving the life of a child with leukemia, the public has mixed feelings about bypass surgery routinely performed on octogenarians. The reason for this disparity of feelings is that when we assess value in these cases, we implicitly apply a metric other than mortality reduction—namely, years of life saved. If we carry this argument further and consider such components of value as the costs of prevention or treatment and the number and ages of persons affected and receiving services, we would probably direct more resources to such measures as prenatal care, provision of car seats for infants, and immunizations. In evaluating value we should also take into account such factors as individual patient preferences and quality of life (as measured by quality of life years saved, for example).

Challenge. Define what it is we want to optimize when we design systems to deliver and pay for health care.

In addition to our lack of focus on what we want to optimize, some of us still believe that there must be a *trade-off* between cost and quality. Although quality is not completely free, after a point there is either no correlation between cost and quality or a negative association. For example, if one looks at the published reports of the Pennsylvania Health Care Cost Containment Council and considers the cost and risk-adjusted outcomes data for cardiac bypass surgery for hospitals, one finds in many cases that the higher the cost, the worse the outcome. Poor quality in health care is certainly more expensive than good quality. One of the problems of traditional reimbursement systems is that they reward both efficient, high-quality performance and costly, low-quality performance. Although the more efficient providers may make more money than the inefficient, this may not force the latter to make necessary changes.

Challenge. Reward high-quality providers and help lower-quality ones to improve. We must realize that as we accomplish this goal, further institutional consolidations may occur and low-volume institutions may close.

COST

The current impetus to examine health care systems in this country comes from the desires of public and private payers to rein in their portion of expenses. These expenses are a function of three elements: price per service, number of services, and intensity of care. Most public and private cost containment strategies have focused primarily on lowering prices. There are several reasons for this approach. First, price regulation is easy. It is accomplished by governmental fiat or by large insurers' market power. Second, basing payments on volume of services smacks of rationing. This technique, though widely practiced in many foreign countries, is anathema to the public in this nation. Finally, regulating costs due to intensity of service is difficult.

Intensity itself has several components. The first is level of service provided. We may ask, for example, whether the patient needs an operation when medication or watchful waiting may provide similar results. Controversies over the most appropriate treatments for angina pectoris and prostate cancer fall into this category. A second component is the coding of the patient's problem. Even though many insurers track frequency distributions of CPT-4 codes by provider, looking particularly for *upcoding,* few follow up on this analysis with actual chart audits to determine codes' accuracy. A third aspect to intensity is the appropriateness of the site of care. For example, we might ask whether an inpatient ought to be in the intensive care unit or on a general floor. Finally, intensity can be viewed as a proxy for the application of technology, defined by the Office of Technology Assessment as drugs, devices, and procedures and the support systems in which they are delivered. Regulating the application of technology is difficult for several reasons. The foremost reason is the absence of a single body with the authority to issue opinions about the cost benefit or cost effectiveness of technology. For example, the federal government has done its best to remove itself from the role of impartial arbiter of technology implementation and evaluation. This abrogation of responsibility was evident when the Reagan administration partially dismantled the aforementioned Office of Technology Assessment and the Clinton administration watched as a Republican Congress cut financial support for the Agency for Health Care Policy and Research after nearly shutting it down. In the absence of a single authoritative body, the legal system has favored plaintiffs in liability suits even when the science supports defendants. Examples range from suits involving silicone breast implants and autoimmune disorders to those involving Bendectin and birth defects. Fear of liability is a potent factor in technology regulation. Finally, withholding technology is akin to rationing, which, as mentioned, is abhorrent to the public.

An example of apparently successful technological control is managed care plans' use of pharmaceutical formularies. The nominal costs of the drugs determine their formulary status, yet little is known about the effects of switching from a nonformulary drug to one on the approved list. Further, the *total* costs of drugs with cheaper purchase prices are not clear; for example, it is not known whether they cause more side effects or require more laboratory test monitoring.

One often cited example of successful rationing is the Oregon Medicaid waiver program. After various constituencies (including those in the medical, political, and religious communities) gave their opinions about which treatments would be efficacious and cost effective for a number of conditions, those treatments were ranked. The state then imposed cutoffs: treatments below certain rankings are not covered. By prioritizing provisions for technology, however, the state covers more beneficiaries than it did before the waiver program began, and the program's total cost has *increased*.

Challenge. Form a consortium of public and private partners with the ability and authority to coordinate technology assessment; the consortium will standardize benefits, and its findings can serve as legal protection to those offering the benefits.

In the public realm, Medicare Part A expenses have rapidly escalated since that program began in 1966. The federal government responded to threats of Medicare Hospital Trust Fund bankruptcy by changing hospital payments from a cost-plus basis to a cost basis to a system linked to patient diagnosis (diagnosis related groups, or DRGs).

As these various measures were failing, more money was put into the fund by eliminating the ceiling on eligible payroll taxes, the fund's principal funding source. When this too failed, the Balanced Budget Act of 1997 moved home health care from the Hospital Trust Fund to Medicare Part B. This shell game merely shifted the financial responsibility for home health services to general revenues, the source of about three-fourths of Part B funds. As more baby boomers become eligible for Medicare and the ratio of working to retired persons continues to shrink, few politically palatable options are left for saving Part A. The proposal that would have the longest and most significant impact on fund solvency is to delay Medicare eligibility. However, this suggestion has been dismissed by a number of legislators as political suicide.

Although Medicare Part B has also experienced financial pressures, its crisis has not been as severe or obvious because payments come largely from general tax revenues. Few beneficiaries realize that in current dollars their out-of-pocket expenses have never been greater. Nevertheless, political pressure to control expenses derives from fears that premiums will need to be increased. Cost-control responses in the past have evolved from using a *customary, prevailing,* or *reasonable* fee schedule to using a resource-based relative value schedule (RBRVS). Although volume-based updates in the RBRVS fees were initially entertained, political pressure by such groups as the American Medical Association eliminated this consideration. The government then stabilized fee costs by redistribution of payments among specialists. However, now that home health care, one of the most rapidly growing components of Medicare Part A, has been shifted to Part B, it is inevitable that costs for Part B will rise considerably.

Challenges. Ensure long-term viability of the Medicare Hospital Trust Fund and stabilize inevitable escalations in Part B expenses. Such changes may require raising FICA, delaying the age of Medicare eligibility, or making each generation responsible for its own expenses, with a safety net for those who cannot afford care.

The other major public health care program, Medicaid, has become a financial burden for both the federal government and individual states. In order to alleviate this problem the federal government began to allow states to obtain waivers to the traditional program. Problems with enrollment, eligibility, patient education, development of provider networks, and payment procedures are some of the shortcomings of many state waiver programs. The Balanced Budget Act of

1997 allows states to establish alternative Medicaid plans without such waivers, yet states will still face these administrative problems. An additional problem is the repeal of the 1981 Boren Amendment, which required states to provide "reasonable and adequate" payments to Medicaid providers. Lacking this federal protection, these providers now face an uncertain process for payment determination. A further important dilemma facing Medicaid is the demographic disparity between eligible recipients in general and those who receive the most program benefits. Although most eligibles qualify for Medicaid because they meet the criteria for Aid to Families with Dependent Children (AFDC), most of the Medicaid money is spent on nursing home care for the elderly. (AFDC was replaced by the Temporary Assistance for Needy Families program in 1996. Those eligible under AFDC prior to July 16, 1996, can retain Medicaid coverage, however.)

Challenges. States need to develop an organizational infrastructure that allows efficient and effective Medicaid management. Rather than use a traditional public health model, they need to borrow the best features of successful managed care plans, including information systems and customer relations programs. They need to provide adequate funding (and timely payment) to ensure participation by a wide network of qualified providers. And they need to establish fairer systems for allocating resources between AFDC recipients and the elderly.

In the private sector during the 1980s and early 1990s, employers faced double-digit increases in their health insurance premiums. Frequently their health care costs approached net profits. In response to these financial pressures, large employer groups engaged in at least three strategies. First, they took advantage of the flexibility in health plan design and coverage afforded by ERISA. Second, they either bought coverage or contracted for administrative services from managed care plans, particularly health maintenance organizations (HMOs). Finally, they shifted more financial responsibility to workers, in the form of higher cost sharing for premiums or of increased coinsurance and deductibles. As part of this shift, coverage for dependents has diminished, perhaps contributing to the size of the uninsured population, particularly children.

Challenge. Make health insurance more affordable to employers and individuals through benefit redesign, appropriate employee cost sharing, and realistic expectations about the trade-offs involved between cost and quality on the one hand and freedom of choice of providers on the other (as discussed later).

QUALITY

The public and private focus on cost-cutting measures is leading people to direct increased attention toward ensuring that quality is not diminished. Briefly, the public is concerned with at least two dimensions of quality: technical and service (that is, amenities of care). Only the former is discussed here. Scrutiny of the technical dimension impels these questions: Are things done for the right reasons? And are they done correctly? Questions policymakers may ask of the public are whether people know how to evaluate the technical aspect of quality, and if so, will their care-seeking behavior change once they know some answers? The response to both those questions appears to be no, at least for now. For example, published risk-adjusted mortality rates for New York State cardiovascular surgeons had little impact on patients' choices. Likewise, the Pennsylvania cardiovascular data mentioned earlier have not been shown to alter patient decisions. One bright spot in this effort is the work of the Foundation for Accountability (FACCT) that seeks to make valid quality measurements understandable to the average health care consumer. This initiative, however, is aimed at allowing comparison between health plans rather than at evaluating individual providers.

A further problem with evaluating technical quality is that services are frequently required emergently. Even if the quality data could be perfectly understood, time is often not available to gather them. And even if a patient knows the best provider, an emergency situation may allow access only to the closest provider.

Challenge. Provide more quality information, make it more understandable and accessible to the public, and improve efforts to make *all* providers better, rather than punishing the bad and improving only the best.

ACCESS

Access to health care has a number of dimensions. The first is being able to afford such care. For many services, being able to afford the care translates into being able to purchase a health insurance policy. Currently about forty-one million people are uninsured in this country. The reasons range from inability to purchase a policy because of a preexisting condition to inability to afford a policy to the gamble that coverage will not be needed.

Having insurance coverage is certainly important, but it is not the whole story behind access. For example, in a November 26, 1997, press release, the Agency for Health Care Policy and Research stated that of the 12.8 million families who faced barriers to health care, just 3.3 million were completely uninsured. Perhaps a more telling statistic from the same study was that more than forty-six million persons lacked a regular source of health care. Similarly, as shown by a Rand Corporation health insurance experiment (Keeler, 1992), out-of-pocket expenses, although reducing utilization, did not have a substantial impact on health outcomes.

Certainly several factors in addition to cost and the ability to obtain insurance influence the accessibility of health care. First is the availability of health care providers. Despite the oversupply of physicians in some metropolitan areas, many inner cities and rural areas lack adequate numbers of practitioners. Several reasons for this disparity exist, including practice conditions and differing rates of compensation. Second, transportation is not always easy for those who need care, even when practitioners are available. This holds particularly true for the poor and elderly. Third, scheduling and coordinating multiple diagnostic and therapeutic procedures can be complex and confusing, even for those familiar with the health care field. Facing these challenges, some may wish to forego even needed services as simple and infrequent as screening mammographies. Finally, understanding insurance benefits and proper filing procedures can be daunting, perhaps causing some to avoid needed services.

Some organized delivery systems have addressed these access issues. They have coordinated services among otherwise fragmented system components, recognized the difference between health care and disease care by offering more preventive services, and moved from an acute care model to a continuum of care model.

Challenge. Enhance coordinated systems' efforts by offering incentives for eliminating waste and improving communitywide health outcomes. Such systems do not have to be under a single owner but can comprise a number of community-based organizations, often those competing with one another.

PARADOXES

The one constant and growing desire among members of the public is to choose their own providers. The public and the press trace the blame for many of the "horror" stories about managed care to closed systems. The common refrain is, "If only this person had been allowed to choose his or her own providers, this wouldn't have happened." Those making such statements believe it is possible to have freedom of choice of providers, high-quality medical care, the best access to such care, and low costs. Unfortunately, all these features cannot be optimized simultaneously. The challenge we face is determining how much of each we want and what trade-offs we are willing to accept in order to obtain the desirable mix.

Freedom of Choice and Access

The best feature managed care has to offer, compared to the traditional fee-for-service sector, is enhanced coordination of services. It is difficult for individuals to coordinate their own care across a continuum of needs. Further, if providers' financial incentives are not aligned, there is little reason for those providers to coordinate care. Witness the traditional Medicare system where one practitioner often hands off a case to another; one person's responsibility ends and another person's begins. In typical managed care systems, however, the primary care physician is responsible for coordinating care regardless of the varied needs the patient has. This process is the essence of case management. Conversely, complete freedom of choice implies that the patient is substantially responsible for coordinating his or her own services. Although managed care plans require primary care providers and medical groups (via contracts and financial incentives) to provide timely care, initial appointment delays often exist. Once their problem has been identified, however, many patients find the referral process better coordinated under managed care than in the fragmented fee-for-service environment.

Freedom of Choice and Quality

As pointed out earlier, in the public backlash against the real and anecdotal abuses by managed care plans, the primary solution one hears is to give beneficiaries freedom of choice of their providers. Some states have gone as far as passing laws making freedom of choice a patient right. For example, Illinois allows a woman to see any contracted obstetrician-gynecologist in the plan, and Florida requires plans to provide freedom of choice of dermatologists. Further, some states have passed what is called *any willing provider* legislation. These laws require health plans to accept any provider willing to sign a standard health plan contract. At the same time these measures are being passed, health plans are designing new *open access* products (discussed further later). These give members the opportunity to see a wider network of providers than they can under a more restrictive HMO product. And all these changes are occurring at the same time health plans and their contracted providers are facing increased external scrutiny and accountability for the quality of care they provide, for example, in the form of National Committee for Quality Assurance (NCQA) certification, Health Plan Employer Data and Information Set (HEDIS) reports, and FACCT criteria. The trade-off with respect to freedom of choice and quality is that we cannot expect accountability in a system where plans and providers lose control of their referral choices and hence of the ability to coordinate care. For example, in Illinois it is not uncommon for OB-GYNs to hospitalize a patient at a facility where her primary care physician and other consultants are not on staff. In these cases freedom to choose an OB-GYN has taken precedence over continuity of care.

Freedom of Choice and Cost

As with costs of other insurance products, health care coverage costs depend on the choice the insured makes to pay either low premiums and higher out-of-pocket expenses (like coinsurance and deductibles) or higher premiums and lower out-of-pocket expenses. With the introduction of managed care plans a third dimension was introduced—freedom of choice of providers. In the prototypical HMO, if the insured receives nonemergency services from noncontracted providers, the plan will not pay for that care. Compared to indemnity insurance, however, the HMO premiums are lower, as are out-of-pocket expenses. For example, traditional HMOs may have copayments, but they do not have coinsurance or deductibles. With the evolution of managed care plans to include preferred provider organizations (PPOs), beneficiaries can have some portion of nonemergency services covered when they receive those services from providers who do not contract with their health plan; however, the insured's financial liability is greater. Also, premiums may be higher for these plans than for HMOs. The insured person has therefore traded more freedom of choice for higher costs. Responding to recent public

147

demand for more provider choice, health plans have created hybrids between HMOs and PPOs called Point of Service (POS) plans. Also, the products called open access plans have emerged. In these pseudo-HMOs, beneficiaries can refer themselves to any plan provider without a referral from their primary care physician.

In this evolution of products the trade-off between premiums, out-of-pocket expenses, and freedom of choice has in many cases been lost. The public has demanded open access products at HMO prices. In order to meet this demand and sustain profits, health plans have shifted the cost of these ill-designed products to providers in the form of lower payments. In the past year many major health plans have experienced unexpected losses. Although a number of reasons exist for this phenomenon, like poor information systems, I believe one of the fundamental causes is the failure to realize that low premiums, low out-of-pocket expenses, and freedom of choice of providers cannot coexist to the extent that health plan marketing has promised. A possible first step to solving the freedom of choice dilemma would be to require all employers who provide health insurance for their employees in the form of an HMO to also furnish a freedom of choice product. The companies would not be required to pay extra for this benefit; the difference in premium would be borne by the employee.

—––—

The public wants access to health care coverage; it does not want to be told where it can receive health care. It wants the best quality care and demands that care be affordable. It is impossible to fulfill all these demands simultaneously. The real challenge for the political process is to determine how we can achieve an optimal mix of those features, satisfy the most, disenfranchise the fewest, and return health insurance to its original purpose—indemnification against catastrophic loss.

References

Agency for Health Care Policy and Research. Press release. Agency for Health Care Policy and Research, Nov. 26, 1997.

Keeler, Emmett B. "Effects of Cost Sharing on Use of Medical Service and Health," *Journal of Medical Practice Management,* 1992, *8,* 11–15.

SECTION FIVE

Preparing for the Global Health Transition

Preparing for the
Global Health Transition

Kent Glenzer
Maurice I. Middleberg

Kent Glenzer currently is director of the Management Technology Unit of CARE, assisting overseas country offices in strategic and operational planning, leadership development, and organizational change processes. Over the past fifteen years, he has worked in seventeen African countries, assisting nonprofit and public sector organizations in strategic planning and strategy implementation, organizational and management development, training, and organizational restructuring.

As director of the Health and Population Unit of CARE, Maurice I. Middleberg has overall responsibility for CARE's family planning and reproductive health program and for integrating family planning and reproductive health into CARE's health, development, and relief programs. He is also an adjunct faculty member at the Rollins School of Public Health at Emory University, where he teaches the Reproductive Health Program Management course.

This is a challenging and exciting time for public health professionals working in the developing world. A demographic and epidemiological transformation is underway, creating a more diversified set of health needs in populations traditionally served by international health care nongovernmental organizations (IHNGOs). This shift will redefine the international public health agenda over the next twenty-five years and require health care leaders to, first, adopt fundamentally new approaches in grassroots health programs and, second, make courageous decisions about organizational mission, strategy, structure, skills, and performance measurement.

THE HEALTH TRANSITION

In the 1960s, mortality in the developing nations was highly concentrated, with more than 35 percent of annual deaths occurring in children under five. These deaths were largely attributable to a relatively constrained set of factors: vaccine preventable diseases, diarrheal disease, respiratory infections, short birth intervals, and malnutrition. By 1996, child mortality was down to 22 percent of total deaths (World Health Organization, 1997), and fertility rates, a proxy for obstetric risk, were down in every region except sub-Saharan Africa.

Enter a very different picture of health problems. *The Global Burden of Disease* (GBD; Murray and Lopez, 1996), a study on which the Harvard University School of Public Health and World Health Organization (WHO) collaborated, reveals that developing world health problems are becoming highly differentiated. Here are the trends that will be important over the next twenty years:

- High levels of fertility, child mortality, and maternal mortality are concentrating in sub-Saharan Africa and South Asia; infectious and parasitic diseases remain the most important cause of death in the developing world.
- Mortality percentages are increasing for older age groups.
- Chronic diseases—including cardiovascular diseases, cancers, and respiratory diseases—have become responsible for almost 40 percent of all deaths in developing nations (World Health Organization, 1997).

- Emerging, reemerging, and drug-resistant infectious diseases—of which the most prevalent are HIV/AIDS, tuberculosis, and malaria—are increasing.

- Mortality data are obscuring the larger and more complex issue of the *burden of disease,* a measure that reflects the impact of diseases that seriously hamper economic productivity and quality of life. Table 1 shows the long term trends in the burden of disease. They indicate that no one package of services will uniformly bring down mortality and morbidity. Instead, the developing world faces a *double burden of disease;* as substantial pockets continue to confront the old enemies of childhood disease, unwanted high fertility, and high maternal mortality, many countries and subpopulations will have to grapple with a very different and new disease burden.

A NEW APPROACH TO PROGRAMMING

Increasingly complex health care needs require new operational realities based on new approaches. The *health security framework* (HSF) is a model we have developed to promote the kind of leadership that can respond to the heterogeneous and evolving health care challenges identified by the GBD Study. Health security is achieved when households identify, prevent, and manage significant risks to the health of

1990	2020
1. Lower respiratory infection	1. Unipolar major depression
2. Diarrheal disease	2. Road traffic accidents
3. Conditions arising during the perinatal period	3. Ischemic heart disease
4. Unipolar major depression	4. Chronic obstructive pulmonary disease
5. Tuberculosis	5. Cerebrovascular disease
6. Malaria	6. Tuberculosis
7. Measles	7. Lower respiratory infections
8. Ischemic heart disease	8. War
9. Congenital anomalies	9. Diarrheal disease
10. Cerebrovascular disease	10. HIV

Table 1. Ten Leading Causes of Disease Burden in the Developing World.

household members. Households accomplish this through healthy behaviors, empowered communities, capable institutions, optimal health technologies, and appropriate public policies. The HSF has seven major components, or elements:

• *Household focus.* The framework explicitly ties health status to the overall livelihood security of a household. Poor families face excruciating choices in allocating scarce resources among health care, food, and other basic needs. It follows that health programming should take place within the context of an overall development strategy that brings multiple, mutually reinforcing interventions to bear on the participating households.

• *Risk analysis as basis for programming.* Risk assessment, which includes indicators of disease burden (years of life lost, years lost to disability, quality-adjusted life years, disability-adjusted life years), is the foundation for programs that can be adjusted in response to shifting epidemiology. Levels, causes, and effects of mortality and morbidity must be disaggregated within and among households as well as between genders and among social groups. It is important to combine the tools of epidemiology with the perceptions of the involved households, given the well-known discord between quantitative and subjective risk assessment. Finally, risk assessment is not the sole province of health experts; it must involve the range of legitimate stakeholders and recognize the legitimate diversity of decision-making criteria.

• *Optimal health interventions.* Associated with major causes of mortality and morbidity are what experience and research tell us are optimal health interventions. As principal health risks change over the coming decades, however, optimal health technologies will also change. It is an open question whether the new problems described in the GBD will be amenable to the same technologies used in the past. IHNGOs can play a useful role in testing alternative technical packages.

• *Healthy behaviors within the household.* Many of the current risks experienced by poor households in the developing world can be mitigated at low cost through changes in behavior at the household level. As the nature of health risks changes, however, the costs, benefits, and effectiveness of behavioral change strategies will change. In addition, a household focus reminds us that healthy behaviors, and the opportunity costs they often represent, must be directed at the concerns of the various household members.

- *Community empowerment.* Community norms, social structures, and leadership influence household health behaviors, both positively and negatively. Creating effective, sustainable community-based organizations (CBOs) that can stimulate institutional and policy change is key to managing the health transition. Building the skills of women's groups to mobilize for health care is particularly important, given the shifting burden of disease.
- *Institutional capacity.* Health security and the management of health risks also require that health institutions have the requisite capacity. We use the term *health institutions* broadly. It includes public, private, traditional, nonprofit, and for-profit providers of health services. Capacity building is an effort to match the skills and systems of health institutions to the most important health problems. It has three dimensions. First, capacity building should facilitate *access* to the services and commodities needed to address current and emerging health risks. Access encompasses physical proximity to needed services and the economic means and sociopolitical liberty to seek those services. Second, capacity building should ensure the quality of services, including the technical competence of providers, adequacy of client counseling, respect for the dignity and confidentiality of the client, existence of client follow-up, and appropriate physical setting for care. Lastly, capacity building must strengthen management systems, including community health assessment, planning, human resource management, monitoring and evaluation, drug and commodity supply, equipment and facilities management, and financial management.[1]
- *Appropriate public health policies.* Public policy influences both the application of appropriate health technologies and the promotion of appropriate health behaviors relative to the greatest risks to health. With disease burden changing, IHNGOs must advocate for a review of public and tacit policies governing health care, to ensure they are consistent with reducing the shifting risks to health.

The HSF is helping CARE field programs that respond to the reality of heterogeneous and constantly evolving health risks. Concomitant with changes in grassroots programming is the need to develop an adaptive organizational strategy that responds to epidemiological transition. This is the first and most fundamental task of the IHNGO leader who wishes to position the organization for the twenty-first century.

THE IHNGO LEADER'S WORK: ORGANIZATIONAL STRATEGY, STRUCTURE, SYSTEMS, AND COMPETENCY

The coming health transition requires IHNGOs to reexamine their organizational mission and role. Such hard thinking must then be translated into explicit strategy. New strategy will require new organizational structures, systems, and competencies.

Strategic Options

The shift in the global burden of disease presents a classic example of market redefinition. The IHNGO that wishes to adapt to the health transition has four generic strategy options, as shown in the simple matrix in Figure 1.

STICK TO THE KNITTING. Two factors might lead an IHNGO leader to adopt the strategy of sticking to the knitting. From a resource perspective, few IHNGOs have the capital to invest in experiments. Given that donor and host government priorities lag behind paradigmatic shifts, the cautious IHNGO leader might consciously choose to remain

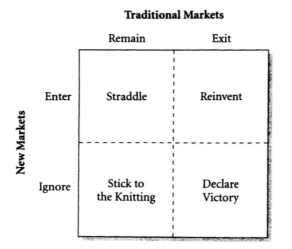

Figure 1. Four Strategy Options for IHNGOs.

154

in current niches. Second, the emerging disease burden will most negatively affect the relatively wealthy while the old enemies will persist among hundreds of millions of the very poor. Remaining in current niches may very well be more congruent with an IHNGO's existing mission and its culture. This strategy is not without risk, however. Organizations that remain in traditional niches may not have markets for their services ten years from now. Within the foreseeable future, traditional IHNGO health care programs will no longer attract significant donor funding: indigenous NGOs, private providers, and host governments will have the capacity to meet health care needs in a more cost-effective manner. An IHNGO leader who selects this strategy will face obsolescence within two decades.

DECLARE VICTORY—AND GO HOME. *Declare victory—and go home* is a sound strategic option. For decades we in this field have said that our goal is to work ourselves out of our jobs; this strategy will hold us to this underlying philosophy. To be an effective strategy, however, it requires the IHNGO leader to implement a rigorous, long-term process of phasing the IHNGO out. The IHNGO will need a small number of key, macro indicators of health status; as these country-specific indicators are met or surpassed, the IHNGO can cease the respective programming and focus resources on an ever-diminishing number of country programs.

STRADDLE. Under the straddle strategy, IHNGOs will adopt a dual track program, continuing to address the enduring problems of child mortality and poor reproductive health and simultaneously developing a more diverse health portfolio. Small and well-monitored pilots will be an important element of such a strategy. Raising awareness of new health care needs among donors and governments will be another key component of a successful straddle strategy. The careful insertion of small leading-edge components within traditional health projects will be yet another. A caveat, however: a straddle strategy that results not from conscious choice but from leaders' simple inability to make hard choices will fail. A successful straddle strategy will also combine elements of the declare victory option, in order to avoid portfolio creep.

REINVENT. IHNGO leaders have a window of opportunity in the next decade to transform their health portfolios. If done well, such a strategy

155

will position the organization for many more decades of valuable work and will result in extraordinary differences in mission and vision. Yet an IHNGO leader who opts to reinvent faces tremendous obstacles.

The investment needed to build competence is high. The reinvent strategy also brings with it a risk of portfolio proliferation, of trying to do everything and doing nothing well. The successful implementation of a reinvent strategy will demand strong leadership, a firm long-term vision of where the organization's health portfolio should be a decade or more from now, and tangible investment in current staff.

Given that the reinvent strategy will likely be attractive to many IHNGO leaders, the remainder of this chapter turns to the challenges to successful strategy implementation.

Structural, Systems, and Competency Changes Required by Reinvention

IHNGOs will need to be structurally integrated into global surveillance and information systems. Health risk management in a rapidly evolving context requires continuous access to epidemiological information. IHNGOs will require a stronger focus on both accessing information from and providing information to the global network. Such structural integration will demand a great deal of time and effort from IHNGO leaders. A second necessary structural change will be radical decentralization: the GBD study reveals the disintegration of monolithic, globally applicable health approaches and the growth of fragmented, localized *micro-markets*. Such decentralization requires decision-making authority close to the customer. IHNGO leaders face a particularly difficult challenge given that their current financial, decision-making, and administrative systems are defensive, more rooted in ensuring compliance than in promoting decentralized initiative. This challenge pales, however, in comparison to the need for sober, clear-headed performance indicators for decentralized operations, an area in which IHNGOs have a genuinely appalling record. Fortunately, there is nothing mysterious or difficult about such indicators; our real challenge is having the courage to hold ourselves accountable for changes in health status and centering reward systems around the measures of change.

Finally, IHNGO leaders face a tremendous competency gap. IHNGO staff have backgrounds in child survival, reproductive health, water and sanitation, and related primary care fields. These were

156

appropriate competencies under the old paradigm of developing world health concerns. It is less clear that they are important for the future.

PRACTICAL IMPLICATIONS FOR IHNGO LEADERS

IHNGO leaders wishing to reinvent their organizations can take six practical steps.

1. *Raise awareness within and outside the organization.* IHNGO leaders will need to devote time and resources to building a critical mass of consensus about the coming health transition and about organizational mission. They should not underestimate the potential resistance to altered mission and must use every available opportunity over the next few years to organize public conversations. Awareness must be extended beyond the organization to donors, local government officials, the poor and vulnerable with whom they work, and local nongovernmental organizations.

2. *Adapt and apply tools for risk analysis.* IHNGO leaders need to encourage the development, adaptation, and implementation of practical tools for assessing and weighting risks. Here we see a marriage among the tools of epidemiology, community participation, and management decision making. Epidemiological data are only inputs into a participatory process that involves all relevant stakeholders. In setting the health agenda all elements of the HSF—behavior, community empowerment, institutional capacity, policies, and so on—should be considered.

3. *Build new skills and reward their use.* Key components in such a strategy are

- Knowledge of emerging health problems
- Skills in participatory approaches to risk analysis, program development, and project monitoring and evaluation
- Knowledge of health security at the household level and skills in applying it
- Capacities to lead institution building and organizational development at the grassroots level

157

- Concrete and visible promotion of innovators (a basic responsibility of organizational leadership), providing them with money, encouragement, and political protection

4. *Select partners for strategic alliances and build long-term relationships.* Given the coming heterogeneity of health problems, it is unlikely that any organization will be able to advance health security without drawing on the skills and resources of other organizations. Strategic alliances will help IHNGOs acquire short-term competence and augment their capital and are attractive to donors and host governments. Strategic alliances are excruciatingly difficult to develop, however; relationships must be nurtured slowly and empathetically, and partners need to decelerate the implementation process if they are to build trust and understanding.

5. *Strengthen linkages with global surveillance systems.* Because of their deep roots in local communities, IHNGOs can play a vital role in building local capacity to carry out surveillance, detect anomalies and trends in a pattern of disease, and feed this information into global systems. This will be a vital function of the twenty-first century IHNGO. IHNGO leaders must also invest in information technology so staff can make more effective use of the global surveillance data.

6. *Design performance indicators, reward systems, and management information systems to meet the health transition.* IHNGO leaders must establish concrete, tangible measures of program performance, overhaul internal reward and recognition systems accordingly, and construct global management information systems that adequately track both organizational and individual performance. At the individual and project level, novel measures are particularly needed for community ability to manage health risks and mobilize around health problems, health institutions' quality of care, effectiveness of advocacy efforts, quality of strategic alliances and local partnerships, strength of linkages between grassroots projects and global surveillance systems, and financial efficiency.

Note

1. CARE has developed an instrument, the Management Capacity Assessment Tool, for assessing management systems. This instrument, which has been applied in countries such as Bangladesh and Haiti, is available upon request.

References

Murray, C.J.L., and Lopez, A. D. (eds.). *The Global Burden of Disease: A Comprehensive Assessment of Mortality and Disability from Diseases, Injuries, and Risk Factors in 1990 and Projected to 2020.* Cambridge, Mass.: Harvard School of Public Health, on behalf of World Health Organization and World Bank; distributed by Harvard University Press, 1996.

World Health Organization. *World Health Report.* Geneva, Switzerland: World Health Organization, 1997.

159

160

SECTION SIX

Nursing in the Next Century

The Future of Nursing

Transforming Nursing Leadership

Nursing in the Next Century

Edward O'Neil

O'Neil closes the book by returning to the assumptions about the future environment RNs will practice in, which are first delineated in his introductory chapter and echoed throughout the book. He predicts that market forces will continue to drive the transformation of service delivery over the next five years. Although there will be some variation across regions as to when the changes will come about, most nurses will increasingly find themselves responding to issues of cost, patient satisfaction, and quality. Health care organizations will be more experimental, which will serve the interest of nurses. O'Neil presents seven broad strategic recommendations for actions, drawn from the more specific findings and recommendations presented in other chapters, that will be key to assuring nursing success in the future. The recommendations include a call for an integrated nursing practice and education continuum, and renewed focus on traditional core competencies of population-based health management and psychosocial interventions. There is also a call for strengthening research in order to demonstrate the efficacy of nursing intervention, building new partnerships, and investing in leadership development.

The chapters of this book paint dramatically variable pictures of the future of nursing practice and education. One is drawn to employ that favorite opening of high school yearbook editors, "it was the best of times, it was the worst of times." As the health care system continues its process of reinvention, all health professionals face both great opportunities and daunting threats from the changes that abound. Labor costs account for 70–80 percent of total health care expenditures. Any effort to change health care will affect the roles, requirements, and working environment of all health care workers.

As health care delivery organizations consolidate and restructure themselves, this new environment will present different career pathways for nursing professionals. At the same time it may also reduce the number of nurses needed in hospitals and other traditional settings. This may create a situation where some nurses with advanced training and skills are widely sought after, while others with entry-level training and experience find it difficult to gain employment. New candidates, such as the multiskilled allied health care worker, may be utilized to perform those tasks traditionally carried out by nurses. As systems strive for efficiency, they will look for every opportunity to substitute unlicensed assistive personnel for licensed professionals for tasks that do not require professional education and licensure.

Nurses' roles and demand for their services also will be shaped by broader demographic, socioeconomic, and scientific trends. As the nation becomes more ethnically diverse, nursing will also need to create opportunities to ensure that the profession represents the nation's population. Although the demographic bulge of the baby boom has yet to reach retirement age, it looms as a reminder that the nation is aging and will increasingly demand health services geared to an older population. The Human Genome project and other biomedical research efforts will continue to yield discoveries that will dramatically alter the prevention, diagnosis, and treatment of illness. Finally, information and communications technologies present enormous opportunities for changing the location, pattern, and structure of clinical practice. Nurses will find themselves in the midst of these and other transitions as well.

Along with growing demands for primary care providers will come new recognition of the availability and skills of nurse practitioners. They will increasingly be called upon to carry out many of the duties and tasks that have been the prerogative of physicians. This will represent an opportunity to make systems of care more affordable and perhaps more responsive to patient care needs and satisfaction, but it may also lead to conflict with physicians over scopes of practice.

As nurses are called upon to perform these new roles, there will be corresponding demands for education to provide newly minted nurses with skills to match these challenges and to retrain nurses who must incorporate these new skills into their professional practice. The opportunities are great, but so are the potential downfalls. If nursing is to flourish in the next century, nursing leaders at all levels must fully understand the nature of the transformation and make appropriate adjustments to educational programs, professional policies, and public laws governing the practice of nursing.

Forecasting changes in today's health care system might be likened to using chaos theory to explain the weather. The general patterns and trends are known, but they are being enacted over a very large-scale environment with tens of thousands of microchanges occurring daily. Collectively these microchanges add up to produce a pattern of weather that varies considerably from area to area and from season to season, yet has a definable and knowable trend. At the same time, it is impossible to predict with exactness what the weather will be tomorrow in any particular location.

Regardless of the difficulty, we should try to assemble what the chapters of this book tell us about the changing health care reality, the current status of nursing, and the likely pathways that will face the profession in the future. The authors' insights and impressions about the changing nature of nursing practice address the organization of care and service, the settings in which care is provided, and the way it has been and will be financed. Some of the perspectives offered here completely parallel one another; others are contradictory. Such is the difficulty in trying to predict the future of the rapidly changing and highly variable health care landscape.

ASSUMPTIONS ABOUT THE FUTURE

The assumptions that follow interrelate and are listed in no particular rank of importance. However, they do follow a certain logic of building on the previous assumption. These assumptions will be followed by seven recommendations for action that are structured around the themes of professional education, professional practice, the health care system, and public policy.

1. *Market and political dynamics will continue to be the dominant forces realigning the system of health care in the United States.* Professional, policy, and community forces will continue to play a role in health care, but will serve to mediate the impact of the market and politics rather than dominate the organization and financing of health care. There will be an expansion of efforts at the state and national level to promulgate a regulatory environment in which the health care market can be both efficient and responsive to public needs.

2. *Most of the health care system will make the transformation to the next generation of service delivery over the next five years.* Even those locations that seem well advanced will continue to evolve new ways to organize the delivery of care. Although this seems to be a rather rapid change for a system that has taken fifty years to develop, in reality these developments build on substantial changes that have already occurred in many parts of the country. Such changes have accelerated as market forces have come to dominate health care.

3. *Specific changes in health care will vary considerably across time, geography, and institutional setting, with urban and suburban settings being the most attractive markets for change.* Today, some areas of the country remain untouched by this revolution. However, as the market in health care becomes more voracious it will undoubtedly arrive in areas where traditional modes of organization and financing are most entrenched. The second generation of movement to managed systems will likely go faster because its leaders can draw upon lessons learned in regions where such systems already dominate. In addition, the consolidation of capital in health care is concentrating resources in the hands of entrepreneurs eager to expand market share.

4. *The emerging market will value services furnished by nurses and others as they make a contribution to three outcomes: controlling costs, enhancing consumer satisfaction, and improving the quality of outcomes.* The relative importance of these factors will vary from market to market, but collectively they will remain

paramount. Most markets are now focusing on cost and patient satisfaction. However, as excess capacity is extracted from the system, the capacity to add value by improving the outcomes with alternative approaches to delivery will become increasingly important. The most forward-thinking health care organizations are already embarking on a health improvement agenda that promises to yield long-term changes in the ways costs are controlled and quality is improved. In any given market, health care organizations will have two kinds of consumers: individuals and large corporate purchasers. These two groups will bring different values and expectations to their encounters with the health care system.

5. *The market will continue to develop and use managed systems of care as the principle mechanisms for making health care more responsive to cost, consumer satisfaction, and health outcomes.* Two major types of managed care plans are emerging in this marketplace. In recent years, there has been considerable growth in those parts of the health care system that represent more open, networked, or virtual systems of care. In these arrangements, managed care companies contract for services with physician groups, hospital systems, home nursing agencies, and other health care providers. The system is a virtual one in that the managed care or insurance company joins those inputs that meet their needs for cost control, consumer satisfaction, and overall quality. The alternative to such an approach is vertical integration, in which a single entity that owns or controls all inputs, such as a staff-model HMO or a provider-owned delivery system, provides a full spectrum of management, professional, and institutional services. Each approach has its strengths and weaknesses. Virtually integrated systems are more flexible, whereas vertically integrated systems are better positioned to standardize clinical and organizational processes. It seems likely that these two approaches will be balanced in the future. Regardless of which strategy is pursued, the health care system will be marked by increased consolidation of providers, both within service groups and across geography.

6. *As systems gain more control over the various inputs necessary to produce health care and as consolidation of health care providers yields fewer options for purchasers (individual or corporate), health care delivery systems will more aggressively experiment with alternative ways to deliver services.* The market values just described will continue to drive systems' goals, but systems will have more freedom to develop innovative and creative alternatives for achieving these goals. As such innovations evolve, there will be both more opportunity for new entities to enter the market and fewer enfranchised prerogatives for institutions and professionals within the system. This new competitive environment will do more to alter the fundamental relationships of these institutions and professionals than anything else in this century.

7. *The changes that are coming about are made possible in large measure by the information and communications technologies that will become available*

over the next decade. Technology is not driving change in health care but rather is a critical tool for implementing change. Information has been at the root of what has kept health care segmented and specialized; the emergent technology may foster its reintegration. The availability of this technology will facilitate system change in several important ways. First, advances in data collection, storage, analysis, and distribution will permit providers to access both individual and population health data during clinical encounters. Second, powerful tools for linking and quickly analyzing large data sets will facilitate more systematic and intensive management from a population perspective than was possible in the past. Finally, the technology will lead to better access to information by consumers, enabling them to assume increasing levels of responsibility for their own health and care.

8. *Intervention by federal and state government policies and professional associations will not stop the transformation of the health care system.* For-profit institutions may not dominate the health care industry, but they do set and will continue to set the standards for efficiency and consumer responsiveness. To remain competitive, community-based and nonprofit institutions will find it necessary to meet the standards set by the for-profits. The best that policymakers can strive for is the creation of a regulatory envelope that protects individuals, encourages the market to work efficiently, and ensures that population approaches to health care are valued and used. Perhaps the best professional associations can do is to help their members understand the emerging system. They will also be useful as they assist members in accommodating to the requirements of this new order and seizing the opportunities it presents. The nursing profession must not succumb to the temptation to resist these inevitable changes in health care. Instead it should actively position itself to play a leadership role in the transformation in order to better serve the public.

SEVEN STRATEGIES TO POSITION NURSING FOR THE NEXT CENTURY

This dynamic environment presents both peril and opportunity for all professions. Some appear better positioned to take advantage of the changes than others. The professions themselves and the associations that serve them can strengthen their position by anticipating as best they can the changing environment and moving their members to respond constructively. Actions professional associations should take include assessing the profession's current roles, developing scenarios for the future, and retooling professional practice and education to prepare professionals for enhanced roles. Some professional associations are already engaged in this work, but much more remains to be done.

165

The movement by the professional pharmacy community over the past decade toward the preparation of clinical pharmacists offers one example of a constructive response by a profession to changes in the environment. During the early 1980s, it became increasingly obvious that the traditional dispensing function of pharmacists would disappear with growing cost consciousness, changes in technology, and potential substitution of other workers. As a result, the professional pharmacy community began asking where on the continuum of care pharmacists added value to patients and systems of service. The profession's leaders broadened the definition of their services beyond the delivery of a pharmaceutical product to include such responsibilities as working with other clinicians to promote effective use of pharmaceuticals, educating patients about their medications, and the direct delivery of services as part of a team of providers when complex patient care needs required a more active role for the pharmacist.

This broadened role for the pharmacist necessitated a revamped and expanded educational program. The proposal met with considerable resistance within the profession and from other interests, such as chain drug stores. The leadership persevered with the reform agenda and today all academic programs have committed to moving to a Pharm.D. degree, with its focus on pharmaceutical care, by early in the next century.

This transition was successful for several reasons that are important to discuss here. First, the movement was born out of a frank and realistic assessment of the environment. Pharmacists did not deny or attempt to halt the dramatic changes in the health care environment. Leadership was also key to the change. Without the commitment of a sizable part of the profession's leaders to push this agenda, it would have met an early and untimely doom. The third and perhaps most critical element of their success was not expecting to receive full endorsement of their ideas from all involved. Rather, the relatively small leadership cadre built a movement that changed much of the expectations of the profession.

By adapting to change rather than resisting it, pharmacy has positioned itself to play a leadership role in the emerging managed care systems. What comparable steps should the nursing community take to improve its position in the coming transition? Historically, nursing has been driven by the vagaries of the health care market. Indeed, nursing education has its roots in turn-of-the-century hospitals' efforts to meet growing demands for services. This focus on immediate needs has yielded a capacity for flexibility unequaled among health care providers, but it has also inhibited nursing's ability to institute long-term changes. Long ago, nursing recognized the need to rationalize the entry into practice and the relationship between levels of training and work. Yet the profession is still burdened with three entry points to practice and general confusion regarding the different roles played by nurses with various levels of education.

Seven distinct ideas emerge as essential for the renewal of nursing practice and education. They represent strategic directions for nursing. As such, they present a broad outline rather than a detailed blueprint for action. They are intended to form a vision within which nursing leaders can implement specific changes at national, state, and local levels.

Create an integrated continuum for nursing practice.

As the nation's largest health profession, nursing will find the impact of changes in the health care system magnified. The profession has prided itself on being a single profession regardless of level of preparation or experience. One of the great strengths of nursing is the common clinical core experience that is a part of all levels of nursing education. Nursing's orientation toward the management of care will increasingly be one of the most-needed elements in the new system. Such an orientation has been possible only because basic nursing education is not specialized.

However, the new system will create more and more opportunities for health professionals who have richer arrays of skills and competencies. Many opportunities in the emerging health care system will demand differentiation, if not outright specialization. Some nurses continue to cleave to the concept that a nurse is a nurse, in part because of their shared introductory clinical experience. This idea must be jettisoned because it no longer serves the patient, the public, the health care institution, or the profession.

Nursing as a profession must begin to work toward a shared articulation of the competencies and likely practice settings for nurses along a continuum of professional practice. What are the core competencies that distinguish an associate from a baccalaureate-trained RN? Have these core competencies been adjusted to meet the changing needs of the health care system and should they be adjusted further if there is movement to create a continuum of practice as indicated here? How does an experienced RN add value differently from that of a newly minted nurse? What are the changes in practice settings and independence of practice that should occur as the nurse moves along an educational and practice continuum? Addressing these matters is hard work and emotionally debilitating for many in the profession, but it is essential to position the profession to add value to the new care delivery systems that will exist in the next century.

The nursing community should identify a continuum for nursing practice. However, if the profession fails to act the health system will impose its own rationalization to meet its changing care delivery needs. In fact, such divisions are already made informally in many settings. Clearly, the common core of clinical skills should be the base upon which all nursing professional roles are built. This core may be represented in the curriculum at the associate degree level and should represent preparation into entry-level positions in the most supervised environments.

167

The nurse emerging from this entry-level position will have many different options to pursue. Some have always been a part of nursing and others are more relevant to the new systems of care. Of particular importance are the roles of the nurse as clinical team leader, mid-level system manager of patients and populations, and deliverer and coordinator of outreach services. It would seem that these roles require different levels and kinds of experience that all build on the clinical core. These practice domains might appropriately be met by the added value of baccalaureate training, but should also be carried out in part by individuals with training in the core disciplines who have demonstrated competence in these areas in a formal manner.

Finally, there are more advanced roles for nurses in clinical and leadership positions. Advance practice nurses are being called upon to carry out more extensive roles in care delivery systems. As these systems create more opportunity for nursing clinical practice, these roles will undoubtedly expand in both inpatient and ambulatory settings. The system also needs nurses with advanced management and systems training in executive leadership roles. Professionally prepared nurses in these positions will be extremely valuable as they build upon their core clinical education and experience and apply it to redesign the delivery of health services.

These clinical service pathways should be structured in such a way as to accommodate lifelong learning of nurses. Convenient exit and reentry points for further training, from entry level through doctoral level study, should facilitate the movement of the nurse along the continuum of nursing practice. This restructuring of nursing is necessary for the profession to take full advantage of the opportunities that the changing health care system presents. Moreover, the profession has the responsibility to respond to these challenges.

Create a continuum of education that supports the practice continuum.

An individual might enter a particular level of nursing practice directly by extending the period of initial training or by returning for more advanced training as opportunity and personal decisions mandate. Today, nursing may have the best internal career ladder among the health professions. But additional work must be done to identify the practice domain and core competencies at each level of nursing practice and training if nursing is to respond effectively to the demands of the emerging health care environment.

In the long run, the profession will be served best by carefully identifying the level of competency needed for effective nursing practice in each role and setting. Nursing education programs must ensure that they are offering a set of experiences that foster these competencies and that they do so in the most effective and efficient manner. In addition, RNs must see themselves as lifelong learners, seeking out opportunities to upgrade and refine their skills. As with nursing practice, the care delivery system may find that direct intervention to train the workers it needs is more efficient than trying to get the attention of educators.

Ultimately, creating parallel continuums of nursing practice and education could mean that the educational process may diverge from licensure. Such a position is often contentious and counterintuitive to the perceived interests of any profession. In fact, the movement to managed systems of care has made most health professions increasingly more defensive about professional ownership of scopes of practice. Such a step would be a bold statement by nursing. It would be an affirmation that the profession had thought carefully and broadly about the changing competencies needed for successful practice in the new health care system. It would also signal that the profession has structured these competencies in a logical developmental sequence and ensure that the educational programs sanctioned by the profession provide the most effective and efficient set of experiences to achieve these competencies. Membership in the profession would be the gold standard for a prospective employer to ensure that an individual possesses the competencies to add value to the health system.

Focus the profession on two core competencies.

The first impulse for the development of an integrated continuum of nursing practice and a complementary educational continuum will be to focus on the clinical core of nursing. This is important and necessary, but not sufficient to reposition the profession of nursing for the next century. Beyond the needed focus on core clinical skills is the identification and affirmation of core competencies that have always been a part of nursing and that integrated systems of care will increasingly demand. Two related competencies seem particularly important: population-based approaches to health and the incorporation of the psychosocial-behavioral perspective into the delivery of care.

Population-based health means moving beyond the provision of treatment services to individuals as they present acute care needs. This approach to health care requires that the individual, practice, institution, or system take as its unit of analysis the whole population. This will require nursing professionals to understand the concepts and tools of epidemiology and apply them in a variety of contexts, ranging from individual patient encounters to the management of complex systems. Such an orientation also means that nursing professionals must have the skills necessary to assess the health of a population and the capacity to develop a set of outcomes or health goals for that population. Additionally, nursing professionals must be able to determine the most effective way to allocate increasingly limited resources to achieve these goals and to lead individuals or organizations in implementing pathways for effective delivery of services.

This approach to population health and the skills associated with it are at the core of the nursing profession. They are drawn from the profession's basic orientation of care rather than cure. They also come from the profession's historical work in large institutions, public health settings, and the community. But these skills and orientations must be adapted to the new realities and demands of integrated systems of care. This will challenge nursing professionals to rethink how they approach case management, manage within institutions, provide clinical care, work with other professionals, and provide leadership for the system.

Of particular importance will be the ability to use effective analytical skills to control costs and improve quality. The intensive work of changing the patient encounter and managing it in a way to achieve lower costs and higher quality must be led by health professionals. Nurses have the opportunity to take up this challenge, but they must demonstrate that they can deliver these results. To do so, nurses will need better education in the application of analytic tools to the management of health care delivery.

In its focus on care, nursing has always incorporated a larger range of perspectives regarding the determinants and outcomes of health than those encompassed by the biomedical model. In particular, nursing has done more than other professions to incorporate the psychosocial-behavioral perspective into a full range of clinical practice competencies. This orientation shapes the ways nurses deliver care to individuals, design and manage institutions, and think about the population values within entire systems of care.

These two core competencies of serving populations and understanding care in the broad psychosocial-behavioral context will be of increasing value to the emerging care delivery systems. The nursing profession, of course, does not "own" these competencies, and other professions have their own ways of demonstrating ability in these domains. The challenge will be for nursing to strengthen nurses' competencies in these domains and demonstrate why they are uniquely positioned to apply these competencies to the delivery of health care services. For the future, nursing practice and education would benefit from pushing their understanding of these values in the context of the new systems of care. The insights derived from such a process should directly inform the educational and practice continuum described earlier.

If movement in this direction is accepted by the educational part of the profession, the temptation will be to add course work in this area to what is perceived as an already crowded curriculum. A better strategy would be to design a set of educational experiences outside the box of the existing program, aggressively tying such a development to the needs of a radically different health care delivery system.

Strengthen the professional commitment to research.

In part, professional identification means a commitment to understanding and advancing a body of knowledge. However, nursing emerged as a practice-driven profession that has assembled its theoretical and research underpinnings in order to understand the phenomena that practice has presented. Although it may have been seen as a weakness of the profession, this precise orientation has led the profession to value the competencies in population health and psychosocial-behavioral matters that are so important to the new approach to health care.

The distinctive competencies of nursing must be advanced by a much more intentional, perhaps even directed, research agenda from the profession. The emerging system of care will value those inputs that can demonstrate a positive contribution to outcomes for both the individual and the population. Individual professionals and entire professions will have to make the case for themselves based on objective, empirical measures of positive contribution to outcomes. Many of these data collection projects will take years to design and carry out. In fact, one refreshing element of the emerging system seems to be an ongoing commitment to experimentation and improvement. But this means that it may become much more important for a profession to control and advance its research agenda than to control the scope of its practice in traditional ways. In fact, one could argue that the future control of scopes of practice will be a function of research in outcomes, not the actions of legislators.

Some research in nursing is already focused on issues of outcomes and evidence-based approaches to improving the health status of patients. However, this research remains isolated within the body of nursing research. Strengthening nursing's knowledge base in outcomes research should be the central concern of the profession.

Reduce the number of nurses educated in associate degree and diploma programs.

Nursing education programs, like all parts of the health care system, expanded over the past thirty years. This expansion was in response to a growing hospital system and the need for nurses to staff these facilities. Not only has that system stopped growing, it is poised for considerable contraction by a reduction in hospital beds and closure of many hospitals. Such changes will inevitably affect the employment prospects for RNs, particularly at the entry level.

Although it is impossible to know the exact nursing skills needed in the emerging systems, it is likely that value will be placed on an efficient pathway for individuals to enter the system. The associate degree provides such an entry point, but affords only a limited basis for professional development. In addition, associate degree programs have emphasized preparation for practice in hospitals, as have the diploma programs that are already vanishing from the nursing education landscape. There simply will be fewer opportunities for RNs educated solely as generalists at the associate degree or diploma level. Adaptation to the emerging environment will require reduction in their numbers.

The baccalaureate degree may offer some additional time to training, but cannot be a substitute for advanced training or experience. Although nursing should value all pathways, it is critical that the profession develop education programs that are flexible, more integrated into the continuum of practice, and able to evolve with both the individual professional and the needs of the care delivery system. Nursing will need to be open to exploring creative alternatives for achieving these goals. The associate-to-master's-degree bridge programs already in operation should be looked to as one approach to addressing these issues.

Create strategic partnerships for nursing.

For the past five decades the U.S. health care system has built a tremendously complex system of care. One of the elements of the complexity has been the segregation of care into discrete professional domains—nursing, medicine, pharmacy—and the separation of processes associated with health into equally discrete institutions—public health, hospital, clinic, finance. What seems likely in the future is that much of what has been separated will be reconnected, particularly when the reunion produces positive system outcomes.

Because nursing is so central to most systems of care, it is in an excellent position to become essential to many of the partnerships that will emerge. Nursing should be strategic in choosing its partnerships. Choices should be made in a way that enhances the ability of the profession to contribute its core competencies in population and psychosocial health. These choices will vary over time and place, but some general alignments of interests seem to be emerging.

In health care delivery, thoroughly integrated systems are likely to make better partners than the parts of the system that still operate independently. A system is able to look across a full range of service needs and has the independence to create innovative approaches to meet those needs. The independent components of a system, such as hospitals, seem more likely to maintain their traditional biases for organization and financing of care and may not have interests that reach beyond their institutional walls. Nurses will find partnerships with such organizations difficult as the missions and strategies of professions and health care institutions move toward further integration. Without an agreement to create something new, nursing educators and hospital leadership will find themselves more often at an impasse than at a creative juncture to reengineer the health care delivery process.

The academic health center has been the leader in health professional education. But this arena has been so dominated by academic medicine that for the most part other professions have not been adequately integrated into these institutions. Moreover, academic health centers face a difficult decade as they redefine their own mission and move to new mechanisms of finance. As nurses look for partnerships for education they might look to the care delivery system or health care plan, as well as to the schools and colleges that have been nursing's traditional partners. Is it wise for the profession to look to the practice world for educational partners after having so recently left the hospital or

172

diploma school for the academic organization? This is a legitimate concern. However, the practice and educational worlds have evolved considerably in the past fifty years, and nursing education and the emerging health care systems have complementary needs and resources.

Research in health professions has grown around the biomedical model funded essentially by the National Institutes of Health. Nursing professionals have made significant inroads into this funding source, and they should continue to develop and carry out projects in this modality. The most promising new research partnerships for nursing, however, are in those areas where their strengths in population health and psychosocial-behavioral health integrate with the interests of the emerging system and where pursuit of these interests can be combined with the clinical research work of nurses. Disease management, demand management, and population assessment are all areas that nursing has demonstrated an ability to address through research. The health care systems themselves are the most likely sources of support for future work in these areas. Nursing researchers should begin working now to develop such partnerships.

Invest in enhancing leadership.

Finally, each of these transformations in health care and nursing will come about only if leaders are present at all levels—national, state, professional, institutional—to identify the opportunities and move the profession toward them. The profession of nursing, along with all of the health professions, is confronted with a stark and unsettling reality. The organization and delivery of care is changing dramatically. Some of the changes will benefit nursing; others are undoubtedly distasteful. The ability of any organized profession to respond to these changes is limited by the traditional values and orientations of the professions and by the essential conservative nature of professional life and values. The nursing profession's dominant mode of response today is an organized, and at times unionized, effort aimed at saving jobs. Though the use of such response is probably inevitable during a time of transition, if it becomes the only response of the nursing profession, it will tend to isolate the profession from decision making about the future of the health care delivery systems in which its members work.

Leadership is the antidote to such reactions. But to be successful it must be informed, developed, and integrated. Informed means the ability to step outside the professional box and see how the world is changing. Not all that is going on in the transition of health care is pleasant, but all of it must be seen and understood for leaders to begin to know how to plan and how to act. But knowing is not enough; leaders must also develop the skills for action. Health care has been a heavily regulated industry that neither valued nor needed entrepreneurial-type action. This is no longer the case; entrepreneurship will be a critical element of nursing leadership in the emerging system. Finally, nursing leadership must be

173

integrated across the various factions within nursing that have historically divided the profession. This division is the greatest single obstacle to nursing achieving the promise of the future that is set out in this book.

The complexity and size of the challenge of changing health care in the United States is daunting and can be defeating for some. As big as this challenge is, it is precisely its magnitude and dramatic nature that create an enormous opportunity for nurses and the nursing profession. But this does not mean nursing will be permitted to defend its turf better and resist change longer. In fact, the opportunity will be seized by those individuals and professions that are quick to see the parallels between the basic values of the new system and the values of their own profession. This book has attempted to produce some insights into those patterns of overlap.

But in the final analysis it will be the leadership of the nursing profession that makes the transformation successful or not. Just as with the pharmacy profession remaking itself, nursing has certain strengths and opportunities as well as certain weaknesses and threats. Will the leadership get caught in the old patterns of relating between nursing and other professions, or will it work constructively to create a new governance and relational basis for the profession? Will the leadership defend what is, rather than create what could be? Will the profession cover up weaknesses and places where it may come up short, or will it have the courage to ask and answer new questions?

Like all of the health professional bodies in the United States, nursing is dominated by the professional association and member governance structure. When there was no bottom line in health care these structures were adequate, because resources were not a concern and no one questioned the authority of the professions to make decisions relevant to their work. The times are and will continue to be different. Now, professional workers must prove their relevance to the mission of the emerging systems of care. They will not prove it through lawsuits and strikes, but by the concerted effort to assess what is important about health care change and to understand how they might relate and contribute to the new patterned ways of practicing. These are leadership questions and issues facing nursing leaders as the profession moves into the next century.

This could be the dawning of a new age for nursing. Achieving this promise will fundamentally depend upon the leaders of the profession from the schools to the associations to the practice settings. May they be equal to this formidable challenge.

The Future of Nursing

Marjorie Beyers

Marjorie Beyers is executive director of the American Organization of Nurse Executives (AONE), an organization committed to developing community-based, integrated health care delivery systems. A Fellow of the American Academy of Nursing, she has published extensively and consulted in the areas of nursing administration and health care quality and has presented over two hundred lectures to hospitals, schools of nursing, and professional organizations across the country.

This discussion of the future of the nursing profession and the continued development of nursing as a profession is based on some assumptions:

- Nursing's rich legacy will propel it into the future. Its history is rich with examples of its mission to improve the health of individuals and communities, take care of the sick and ill, and attend to people in times of disaster, war, and crises.

- Future patterns of nursing care will blend past practice into future practice. Nursing's existing mission and values will continue to drive practice, and the way nursing care is delivered will reflect changes in the way the public uses nursing and health care services.

- The nursing profession will undergo significant development in the ways it meets its accountabilities to the public, both in practice and in methods for voluntary credentialing and taking professional accountability for practice outcomes.

- Nursing practice will be aligned with patient requirements for care in health care service sectors that incorporate the continuum of care. Practice will be enhanced and expanded as a result of technological developments in both health care and communication that will increase the use of nursing's capacity to provide patient care.

- The educational preparation of nurses will continue to provide opportunities for career mobility and expanded roles. Nursing will continue to be a unique profession with a growing science but will interface with other health professions in its educational processes. Continuing education will be as important as the basic educational program.

- The nursing workforce will continue to be pluralistic. Shifts in generalization and specialization will occur as patient demand and health care technology develop. Increased patient involvement in care and interdisciplinary care teams will influence staffing and thus workforce requirements, driven by patient demand for care.

- Public policy toward the nursing workforce will be based in newly devised supply-and-demand projection models that incorporate not only patient demand for care but also use of interdisciplinary team collaboration.

FUTURE PRACTICE

The mission of nursing and its values will remain constant, but its delivery modes and location of care will continue to change significantly. In the future, nursing services will be organized around the patient population groups found in three main settings—primary care centers, specialty care centers, and community service centers—connected through governance and administrative structures.

Primary care center nurses, working with health care teams, will provide patient assessment, education, and support with the goal of wellness. Primary care centers will be the basic level of health care for individuals and communities. This cadre of nurses will be responsible for clinical integration of care across the continuum of care and will coordinate each patient's care in collaboration with physicians and other health professionals. These nurses will work with comprehensive data banks containing information on patients' genetic assessment, health history, significant lifestyle factors, and estimation of health risk. The data will also include each patient's chronological record of health care with outcomes. One accountability of this group of nurses will require working collaboratively with physicians and other health professionals to systematically analyze patient data in order to discover ways to improve all aspects of patient care and to learn about causes and effects.

The nursing care role will involve care management over time for individual patients to ensure that assessments are timely and that follow-up is implemented. Primary care nurses will work with health care teams, connecting patients with the other types of care resources as needed. For example, individuals requiring diagnosis and complex treatment will be connected with physicians. Individuals with housing and daily living problems will be connected with community services. The health care team will comprise nurses, physicians, pharmacists, nutritionists, physical and occupational therapists, and rehabilitation specialists, available as needed by the patients. In addition, patients with similar problems and concerns will receive certain types of care in groups. Nurses responsible for a given patient population group will assess the care needed by that group. Members of the interdisciplinary care team will participate in group care as indicated by the group problems. The team, including nurses, will be responsible for the efficiency and effectiveness of care, using electronic communication and quality improvement methods (Parsons, Murdaugh, and O'Rourke, 1998). The nurses will also interface with other components of the health care system, including specialized care centers and community care services.

Specialized care center nurses will be associated with health care centers such as acute care and long-term care facilities, home care programs, and hospice and healing centers. In locations with high-density populations, each care center may be a separate entity, but in areas with fewer people, specialized care centers may be grouped in one facility. Care center nurses' roles will be similar to today's nursing practice. Leaders and clinical specialists will manage the organizational aspects of care and provide direct patient care. Specialized care center nurses will be responsible for the care environment and care management. Interdisciplinary teams will provide comprehensive care, with the nursing role focused on twenty-four-hour care and ongoing care management. The nursing staff will include chief nurses, advanced practice nurses, generalist nurses, and assisting staff. Although these care centers will look much like hospitals of today, they will be designed to meet patients' specialized needs and will be equipped accordingly. Some will be more like hotels, and others will resemble today's high technology hospitals. As in all types of care centers, patients will be actively involved in their care programs. The specialized care center nurses will interface with both primary care and community care nurses.

Community care nurses will be a blend of today's public health nurse, community health care center nurse, and health planner-educator. Community health assessments, plans for improving health, and special projects to deal with selected issues of the environment and ecology will be their main accountabilities. Clients will include community leaders (in schools, churches, businesses, and the other types of groups in which people cluster) who are undertaking special projects to improve the environment for health, to deal with particular health issues, to garner resources in times of crises, and to promote and support neighborhood health groups. Thus community care nurses will often accomplish their work as part of project teams. Community members will participate in designing and implementing projects. One of the important interface groups for community care teams will be the public officials, police and firefighters, and persons whose work brings them into close contact with the grassroots community members (Parsons, Murdaugh, and O'Rourke, 1998). The community care teams will also work closely with the primary care teams, to provide services and support for the chronically ill, elderly, and disabled persons who need assistance. They will work hand in glove with the primary care teams in community-based care centers.

FUTURE ARCHITECTURE

In the future the architecture of the nursing profession will be designed to incorporate the components of education, practice, administration, policy, and research. Because care will be delivered in clinical organizations with less infrastructure than today's organizations have, key relationships within nursing will evolve around education, research and development, and new ways of practice. The profession will have a common core of activities for continued development of its science, evaluation, and improvement. Education, research, and regulation will be specialized functions associated with universities, institutes, and virtual groups sharing the same specialties. Each nurse will develop a professional career profile in each of the five basic dimensions of nurses' professional role: education, practice, administration, policy, and research. Professional leadership will be provided by nurses with doctoral degrees in one aspect of the full professional role. These nurses will be closely associated with professionals in other disciplines who share their areas of focus.

Educators will specialize in delivery of basic and continuing education and will provide expertise in educational interventions for individuals and community health initiatives. They will be conversant with cognitive patterns and theories of learning. They will use new technology to deliver education, designing curricula that can be used in local areas. They will coach and guide others in the use of learning materials and in educational processes.

Administrators and executives will focus on resources and organization. They will participate in the organizational design and operation of patient care delivery, ensuring that structures for patient care are relevant to patient requirements. They will focus on design, decision making for effective use of resources, competency, and outcomes. They will also engage in continual study of care delivery and outcomes, technology assessment, and development of ways to detect when changes should be planned and introduced. They will manage change and work with broad-based teams in all sectors of health care.

Policy experts will continue to be a major force in analyzing public need for quality patient care and in ensuring that policy fosters health for all citizens. Nursing's policy experts will contribute to international, national, and state policy initiatives in unique ways evidenced in patient care. To fulfill a strong patient advocacy role, nursing will establish a learning loop from the care experience to the policy table.

Researchers will continue to develop the science. They may be aligned with specific types of practices, and their research priorities will be to advance nurses' capability to provide quality patient care. Part of their role will be to make research findings accessible to practicing nurses, facilitating application of research to practice.

FUTURE WORKFORCE

Nursing's future architecture includes a design of relationships among the members of the nursing profession workforce and among nurses and the members of other health care workforces. In the future there will be a shift toward higher qualifications, new staffing configurations, and more explicit clarification of the roles and functions of nurses in relation to their educational preparation. In the future the nursing workforce projections will concentrate on qualifications to meet patient requirements for care rather than on numbers in a staffing matrix. Nurses will have more uniform preparation in the respective undergraduate and graduate programs. Graduate preparation will be required for practice in complex situations requiring extensive planning, negotiation, discovery, and analysis in decision making (American Organization of Nurse Executives, 1997, 1998). Higher degrees will be necessary for effective collaboration with other nurses and other health professionals for health care service design, delivery, and evaluation.

Undergraduate preparation will be essential for nurses who wish to specialize in care processes in highly defined situations. These nurses will participate in interdisciplinary care teams and participate in management of care resources to ensure efficient and effective care. The majority of them will practice in specialized care centers, working with patients experiencing acute illnesses or requiring support in managing chronic illnesses. Nursing assistants will provide support for nurses in these sectors. In the future, patients and their families or other personal caregivers will also be active participants in patient care.

FORCES SHAPING NURSING'S FUTURE

Of the many strong forces now shaping health care, four have special implications for nursing's future: the unbundling of health care organizations, the capabilities of health care and communication technology, the development of integrated care delivery systems, and the growth of consumer involvement.

The unbundling of health care delivery into many more organizations and settings than before is setting the stage for future health care. The current redesign, reorganization, and restructuring in health care organizations is being driven by multiple events, including health care financing changes, quality improvement initiatives, and shifting resources. However these events are overshadowing events of greater continuing importance such as the development of health care technology and communication. New technologies and means of communication will eventually be viewed as a pathway to new definitions of care (Hiebeler, Kelly, and Ketteman, 1998). And technological and communication changes will be seen as necessary to keep the growing bureaucracy in health care from restricting development of clinical services useful to patients.

The emerging models of health care delivery have great potential for using nursing's capacity for care. Technology is often overlooked as a major force in health care change, yet it remains the one constant that allows and supports new care delivery methods. Technology can be viewed as supporting or enabling change or as a source of change. Both views have merit. Technology has enabled much of the health care reorganization to date. The increased volume of outpatient surgery, for example reflects advanced health care technology that permits less invasive procedures and shorter patient recovery times. Ongoing introduction of new technology has also changed people's perspective on continuing education. Learning new competencies is now an accepted norm, to keep up with the change.

Technology will continue to mature in ways that will make today's health care system seem primitive. Work now under way in genetics promises to yield genetic diagnostics for detection of specific diseases, treatments using gene-based pharmaceuticals, and genetic therapies. Health care will continue to be challenged by ethical and moral dilemmas created by genetic interventions. At the same time, high-technology lifestyles will create needs for caring services. Healing centers and many of the healing methods used in the past will continue to gain prominence in society as health care is expanded to holistic care.

Introduction of new communication technology is also affecting nursing practice. Nurses along with other health care professionals now provide care through telemedicine, which connects specialists, nurses, and patients in their different settings. Interactive television can also be used to support patients in their home settings. Another example of technology use is *ask-a-nurse* service. These telephone arrangements began as triaging services, were used for marketing, and now are again being used for patient teaching and counseling and also early initial assessment and referral. Many people now use the Internet to obtain information about their illness or disease, information formerly available only to health professionals. As a result, health care professionals must adapt patient information and counseling to the patient's knowledge base. Nurses are using computers to obtain resource information, transmit patient reports, and make arrangements for patient care. Communication technology also enables seamless care; patient records can be transmitted to multiple settings, thus saving time and travel, and more important, enabling decision making. All these innovations influence the way nurses establish patient relationships, design patient education, and participate with others to manage care.

The development of integrated care delivery systems is tapped into nursing's strengths in patient care. The nursing perspective on integrated care delivery is the continuum of care, that is clinical integration of care processes. Nurses understand the continuum of care, and they have processes in place to coordinate care over time and among health care settings. The nursing process, nursing care plans, and clinical pathways contribute to managing care and are used in most care settings. As organizational structures are consolidated and redundancy is reduced, clinical processes become more visible (Institute of Medicine, 1998).

Consumer involvement has been instrumental in making the health care environment more user friendly. In nursing practice, consumer awareness is resulting in an emphasis on service and increased patient participation in care (Morath, 1997). Practices that increase patient satisfaction with service have to some extent replaced previous restrictions on what patients could or could not do, should or should not know. The environment for care is now more conducive to patient involvement in decision making and also facilitates the helping relationship. In this new environment there will be a new focus on the patient and on meeting patient needs across the continuum of care. One of the outcomes is that patients will have more choices about their care. In many instances these choices will be beneficial, but patient choice will also raise new ethical and moral issues, particularly when a patient refuses care known to be helpful. A strong benefit of increased consumer participation in care is that health care team members will become increasingly interdependent.

Another effect of increased consumer choice is the ongoing resurgence of healing remedies from the past, the establishment of healing centers, and the use of non-Western interventions like acupuncture. Nursing science has incorporated many of the *alternative* therapies and documented that such interventions enhance patient outcomes.

FOUR INITIATIVES

Four major initiatives will be prominent in nursing's journey toward the future. They include nursing professionals' relationships with physicians and other health professionals, the way the profession meets its accountabilities to the public, the composition and development of the nursing workforce, and the adaptation of nursing science to changing practice.

Nursing will not be alone in making changes in these areas, and turf battles about overlapping areas of practice and primary accountabilities will increase during the transition. Prescription privileges will be debated, for example. These battles will lead to the charting of new territory as practices and the complementary roles of the various health profession change, and who does what in the new practices is sorted out. In the future, patients and communities will initiate much of their care and will have access to many interventions now managed by health professionals (Center for Health Leadership, 1997). Health care professionals will increasingly be called upon for counseling, guidance, support, and assistance with decisions about health care. Not all professionals will be comfortable with patients' increased control.

The way nursing now meets its accountabilities to the public is largely centered on licensure, certification, and accreditation of services, agencies, and facilities—activities grounded in peer review and expert judgment. Nursing has already begun to consider standards of care across hemispheres, develop multistate compacts for licensure, and organize certification programs through the American Board of Nursing Specialties. These initiatives will converge into a unified approach to monitoring and evaluating the competence of nurses in areas of practice and quality of care. A new structure for professional regulation will emerge. One feature will be a unified focus on entry to practice based on educational preparation, and another will be increasing use of specific competency certification for selected areas of practice. Nursing will also be engaged in the effort to define specialization and generalization in practice. Centralized data banks will contain nurse profiles with data on individuals' basic education, certification, and practice outcomes. Issues of confidentiality, practice opportunities, and useful evaluation will be paramount in determining how the data banks will be used.

The composition of the nursing workforce is varied and complex. Struggles to define the education required for entry to practice and the appropriate education for advanced practice have dominated the field in the past decades (National Advisory Council on Nurse Education and Practice, 1997). In the future, nursing will become comfortable with its pluralism. The profession will continue to include nurses with different types of education, from the basic short-term course to the doctoral program (American Association of Colleges of Nursing, 1998). The trend will be toward eventual consolidation of the baccalaureate and master's programs, however, with associate degree programs preparing nursing assistants, baccalaureate and master's degree programs preparing clinical nurses, and doctoral degree programs preparing nurses with advanced, specialized knowledge. But diversity will continue because nursing will be in the mainstream of education and will be shaped in part by educational opportunities. Adding to the current pluralism in nursing will be the access to self-study and advanced preparation through virtual education on-line. Problems with program availability will be resolved by these virtual programs.

The nursing workforce will be profoundly affected by the trend toward interdisciplinary care. Basic curricula will become more broad based. Schools may develop a core health professional education that is followed with specialized education for a specific discipline such as nursing. This could make more nursing education a master's degree endeavor. In addition, the health professions can be expected to regroup according to patient requirements for care and technology. In the future there will be basic health professions such as physician and nurse and a number of technical programs that prepare these professionals for specific care functions. All the professions will grapple with their identity, their science, and their continued research and educational functions.

The adoption of new science into practice will be equally challenging because in a virtual society many of the quality controls and methods once used to test new practices will not be relevant. Nurses

184

will have access to new information more quickly and will adopt new technology more routinely. The former dependence on rules, regulations, and policies will be replaced with a strong orientation to the ethics of practice, to working in communities of health professionals, and to discerning the effectiveness of care practices through outcomes measurement and analysis. The greatest challenge will be deciding how to deal with process and structure in this outcomes evaluation, because diversity in the ways care is delivered will only increase in the future (National Institute of Nursing Research, 1998). A new way of defining accepted behaviors will include process and structure, with focus on appropriate practices. Increasingly, standards of practice will be developed and adopted worldwide (Commission on Graduates of Foreign Nursing Schools, 1996).

References

American Association of Colleges of Nursing. *Enrollment and Graduations in Baccalaureate and Graduate Programs in Nursing.* Washington D.C.: American Association of Colleges of Nursing, 1998.

American Organization of Nurse Executives. *The Evolving Roles of Nurses in Executive Practice.* Issue brief. American Organization of Nurse Executives, 1997.

American Organization of Nurse Executives. *Refining the Art of Nurse Executive Practice.* American Organization of Nurse Executives, 1998.

Center for Health Leadership. *Exploring Alternative Futures.* Berkeley, Calif.: Center for Health Leadership, Western Consortium for Public Health, 1997.

Commission on Graduates of Foreign Nursing Schools. *The Trilateral Initiative for North American Nursing: An Assessment of North American Nursing.* Philadelphia: Commission on Graduates of Foreign Nursing Schools, 1996.

Hiebeler, R., Kelly, T. B., and Ketteman, C. *Best Practices: Building Your Business with Consumer Focused Solutions.* Simon & Schuster, 1998.

Institute of Medicine. *Primary Care: America's Health in a New Era.* Washington D.C.: National Academy Press, 1998.

Morath, J. (ed.). *Patients as Partners.* Chicago: American Hospital Association, 1997.

National Advisory Council on Nurse Education and Practice. *Report to the Secretary of the Department of Health and Human Services on the*

Basic Registered Nurse Workforce. Rockville, Md.: U.S. Department of
Health and Human Services, Health Resources and Services Administration, Bureau of Health Professions, Division of Nursing, 1997.

National Institute of Nursing Research. *Community Based Health Care:
Nursing Strategies.* Washington D.C.: National Institutes of Health,
1998.

Parsons, M. L., Murdaugh, C. L., and O'Rourke, R. A. *Interdisciplinary Case
Studies in Health Care Redesign.* Gaithersburg, Md.: Aspen, 1998.

Transforming Nursing Leadership

Marilyn P. Chow
Janet M. Coffman
Robin L. Morjikian

Marilyn P. Chow is vice president, patient care services, at the Summit Medical Center, and dean for clinical affairs, at the Samuel Merritt College in Oakland, California. She is program director for the Robert Wood Johnson Executive Nurse Fellows Program, a leadership development program, and she serves on several advisory boards, including the Division of Nursing's National Advisory Council on Nurse Education and Practice.

Janet M. Coffman is associate director for workforce policy and analysis at the University of California at San Francisco Center for the Health Professions. She serves on the advisory committee for the California Strategic Planning Committee for Nursing, and her publications include Strategies for the Future of Nursing *(coedited with Edward O'Neil, 1998).*

Robin L. Morjikian is deputy director of the Robert Wood Johnson Executive Nurse Fellows Program at the University of California at San Francisco Center for the Health Professions. She also oversees other leadership development activities of the center's Training and Consulting Division, including a program for physicians.

Change has been the one constant in health care in the United States in the 1990s. Although the pace and characteristics of this change vary significantly, certain general patterns have emerged in virtually every region across the nation. Since the early 1990s, private and public purchasers have looked to managed care organizations to enhance the value of their health care dollars. The growth of managed care has in turn prompted increased competition and consolidation among health care providers.

These new dynamics have fostered the growth of for-profit organizations, which have set new standards of efficiency by lowering costs while achieving patient outcomes as good or better than those attained by their not-for-profit competitors. Success in this environment requires health care organizations to improve work efficiency, with focused attention to the concerns of increasingly assertive and sophisticated consumers. These developments are facilitated in large part by information technology advances that are expanding access to information for both providers and consumers (O'Neil, 1998).

As a consequence the field of health care has become increasingly complex and chaotic. Health care organizations are constantly revisiting the range of services they offer and the means by which they furnish these services. In effect, the system is requiring leaders and professionals to master the new roles and responsibilities needed to fly an airplane that is being designed and constructed while it is in flight.

The authors gratefully acknowledge the contributions of Janis P. Bellack, Senior Fellow, University of California at San Francisco Center for the Health Professions, and senior consultant to the Robert Wood Johnson Executive Nurse Fellows Program, for her contributions to this chapter. We also thank Edward O'Neil, Catherine Dower, Beth Mertz, and Jean Ann Seago for their helpful comments during the chapter's preparation.

The ramifications of these and other developments are especially pronounced for registered nurses because theirs is the largest health care occupation in the United States, with 2.1 million active practitioners in 1996 (Moses, 1997, p. 33). Consequently, many efforts to improve efficiency involve changes in the configuring of the nursing workforce. The most dramatic reconfigurations are occurring in hospitals, the institutions that employ the largest numbers (60 percent) of the nursing workforce (Moses, 1997, p. 45). Decreasing health care dollars and challenging clinical imperatives to reduce patient length of stay in spite of increasing patient acuity require hospital executives to reevaluate the work of registered nursing personnel. Hospital executives are increasingly challenged to ensure that the right person delivers care at the right time for the right cost. One result is that the role of the registered nurse must focus on tasks that can be performed safely and effectively only by licensed professionals.

Several additional factors compound the challenges facing nursing leaders. First, nursing is probably the most diverse health profession. Multiple points of entry into practice and multiple pathways for career development make it difficult for nurses to reach consensus on appropriate roles for members of the profession. Second, nurses tend to view health care exclusively from the clinical perspective. They are excellent at identifying and responding to the multiple factors that affect the health and healing of individuals and their families, but are not accustomed to considering the economic, political, and social factors that affect health care organizations. Third, the nursing workforce is aging, prompting concerns, particularly among hospital nurse executives, about the system's ability to retain sufficient numbers of experienced registered nurses in increasingly demanding inpatient settings (Fralic, 1998). Finally, in many organizations, turnover among nurse executives is quite rapid, which compromises continuity and generates tension in the relatively stable workforces they are called upon to lead.

PERSPECTIVES FOR SUCCESSFUL NURSING LEADERSHIP

These rapid and dramatic changes in nurses' roles and responsibilities are generating much disruption and anxiety among nurses. Yet they are simultaneously providing nurses with greater opportunities to develop new and cost-effective models of improving the health and well-being of individuals and their communities. One of the most important contributions nursing leaders could make today would be to articulate a coherent vision of the future of both the profession and the health care delivery system. To do so, leaders will have to adopt three complementary perspectives:

Focus on core values

Welcome change as opportunity

Adopt a cosmopolitan outlook

Focus on Core Values

The nursing profession has a strong set of core values that emphasize concern for consumers' needs. Collins and Porras's observations (1997) about successful organizations suggest that nursing would do well to focus on preserving those core values: "Those who build visionary companies wisely understand that it is better to know WHO YOU ARE than where you are going—for where you are going will almost certainly change" (p. 222). This perspective is especially critical in health care today, where the pace of change is rapid. The nursing profession will serve the public best if it concentrates on maintaining and articulating its core values in the wake of these changes.

Welcome Change as Opportunity

However, nursing leaders must not confuse preserving core values with preserving specific roles and staffing patterns. Nursing has an exquisite challenge to educate, mobilize, and motivate a huge, diverse workforce to be flexible and to be welcoming of the ever changing demands of a system in the midst of chaos. Striving to preserve a status quo that will inevitably disappear diverts nursing leaders' valuable energies from creating the profession's future. Rather the nursing leader must become a *transformational* leader, one who "willingly lets go of old patterns and assumptions, and invites new thinking and behaving" (Kohles, Baker, and Donaho, 1995, p. 275). Transformational leadership requires a vision of the future and the capacity to articulate and implement innovative, coordinated strategies to achieve it.

Adopt a Cosmopolitan Outlook

Maintaining core values while looking toward the future will require nursing leaders to broaden their focus. Rosabeth Moss Kanter has observed that traditionally leaders succeeded by concentrating on the interests of their own profession or organization. The new environment in health care requires *cosmopolitan* leaders, ones "who are comfortable operating across boundaries and who can forge links between organizations" (Kanter, 1996, p. 91). This competency is consistent with Murphy's finding (1996) that exceptional leaders "provide a larger structure within which individuals and teams come together to achieve a whole greater than the sum of its parts" (p. 223).

Cosmopolitan leadership in nursing calls for greater engagement at three levels:

Among professional nursing organizations

With other health professionals

With leaders outside health care

PROFESSIONAL NURSING ORGANIZATIONS.   Nurses have organized themselves into myriad professional organizations, each with a different mission and agenda. The American Nurses Association seeks to represent all registered nurses, but the growth of specialty and role-based organizations (for example, the American Association of Nurse Anesthetists and the American Organization of Nurse Executives) suggests that many nurses display greater allegiance to such organizations than to the profession as a whole. At this critical juncture the nursing profession cannot afford such fragmentation because it impedes nurses' ability to reach consensus about the profession's future. Initiatives such as the National Federation of Specialty Nursing Organizations and the Nursing Organization Liaison Forum, which aim to unite nurses around overarching professional issues, must be expanded.

OTHER HEALTH PROFESSIONALS.   Nursing leaders must also work more closely with leaders in other health professions. Enhancing the cost effectiveness of clinical care will require all health professionals to work collaboratively to improve efficiency and patient outcomes. Collaborative leaders also serve as important role models for health professionals in the growing number of organizations that employ interdisciplinary teams to deliver services. In addition, forming common cause with leaders in other health professions to address policy issues of mutual concern will increase nursing leaders' ability to promote legislative and regulatory reforms.

191

LEADERS OUTSIDE HEALTH CARE.   Finally, nursing leaders must also engage more frequently and systematically with leaders outside health care. Building and sustaining healthy communities requires health professionals to look beyond the walls of their institutions to the communities in which they operate. Dialogue with leaders outside health care is critical to identifying community needs and the roles that health care organizations can play in meeting them. In addition, many ideas for innovation are likely to come from those not bound by traditional assumptions about health care delivery.

STRENGTHENING LEADERSHIP DEVELOPMENT

The new dynamics of nursing leadership necessitate a recommitment to educating nurses for leadership roles and a rethinking of traditional patterns for teaching leadership skills. New and complementary strategies, particularly executive-level initiatives, are needed to ensure that nursing leaders acquire needed competencies.

The Need to Develop Executive Leaders

Given the nursing profession's unique position in the health care system, development of strong executive leadership is a paramount concern. Most nurses in leadership positions have been taught leadership only as part of their basic nursing education. At that time, however, they have no professional experience upon which to reflect. They can only absorb general principles and observe the actions of other nurses in leadership roles. As a consequence, many are unprepared for their later leadership roles and responsibilities.

Nurses' frontline roles in care delivery provide them with intimate knowledge of clinical operations. From this experience, they also gain a number of competencies critical to leadership, including cultural awareness, community focus, and conflict management and teamwork skills. However, experience alone is not sufficient to augment the nursing leadership courses taught at the basic level. Nurses require additional leadership competencies if they are to meet the challenges of institutional transformation and system change. In particular, they need a systems perspective and competencies in developing strategic visions, risk taking, innovating, and managing change.

192

Ultimately, leadership development must be conceived as a lifelong process that encompasses multiple episodes of formal training that build upon prior professional experience. Individuals do learn from their experiences, but formal leadership development programs facilitate focused self-assessment and mastery of new leadership competencies.

The Benefits of Leadership Development Programs

A number of formal professional development programs have been established for nurses. Some programs seek to enhance nurse executives' management and business skills. An example of this approach is the Johnson & Johnson–Wharton Fellows Program in Management for Nurse Executives. Launched in 1983, this intensive three-week summer program is geared toward giving nurses an understanding of the personal and organizational dynamics of decision making. It covers such topics as marketing, organizational behavior, the economics of health care decision making, financial management, and mergers and acquisitions.

Such business and management-oriented programs are quite valuable but must be complemented by initiatives that focus on leadership competencies. Executives need more than strong business skills to lead health care organizations in these turbulent times. They must also be able to manage change and communicate their vision of the future to employees, members, consumers, and community leaders.

Recognizing this need, nursing organizations have established programs and initiatives that emphasize leadership competencies, including the Center for Nursing Leadership, which is a partnership of the American Organization of Nurse Executives and the Network for Healthcare Management. The Center for Nursing Leadership enhances executive nurses' leadership effectiveness through a series of experiences such as the Journey Toward Mastery, a yearlong leadership program. Two other initiatives are Sigma Theta Tau's Leadership Institute and the American Association of Colleges of Nursing's Executive Development Series, which includes the Academic Leadership Workshop.

One of the newest leadership development programs for nurse executives is the Robert Wood Johnson (RWJ) Executive Nurse Fellows Program. Sponsored by the Robert Wood Johnson Foundation and directed by the Center for the Health Professions at the University of California at San Francisco, this three-year fellowship program is open to outstanding nurses in executive roles in health services (including patient care services, integrated delivery systems, health plans, and other health care organizations), public health, and nursing education. The program aims to prepare participants for leadership roles at the highest echelons in health care.

Building on the leadership profile advocated by the leadership experts who call for greater collaboration and innovative partnerships, the RWJ Executive Nurse Fellows Program focuses on five key leadership competencies for the next century:

- *Self-knowledge:* the ability to understand self in the context of organizational challenges, interpersonal demands, and individual motivation

- *Strategic vision:* the ability to connect broad social, economic, and political changes to the strategic direction of institutions and organizations

- *Risk taking and creativity:* the ability to transform self and organization by moving outside traditional and patterned ways of success

- *Interpersonal skills and communication effectiveness:* the ability to translate strategic vision into compelling and motivating messages

- *Managing change:* the ability to continually create, structure, and effectively implement organizational change

These five competencies are the program pillars and will infuse the learning experiences of each Fellow. Once appointed, each Fellow will follow a three-year course of study, completing a core leadership curriculum and an individual learning plan and being mentored by a senior executive. Each program component will promote acquisition of the five key competencies. The core curriculum will provide a solid grounding in leadership theory and techniques. The structured mentoring experience will nurture competencies in alliance building, partnership development, communication, and change management through one-on-one interaction with senior executives in various industries. Self-directed activities like peer coaching and journal writing, critical components of the individual learning plans, will foster each Fellow's increased self-knowledge and greater awareness of personal leadership style.

One of the unique features of the program is that it will engage the participating Fellow's employing organization as the Fellow completes a leadership project in that institution. Finally, the program is committed to creating and sustaining an ongoing leadership network composed of current and former Fellows, past and present mentors, faculty, scholars, and other leaders.

References

Collins, J. C., and Porras, J. I. *Built to Last: Successful Habits of Visionary Companies.* New York: Harper Business, 1997.

Fralic, M. F. "How Is Demand for Registered Nurses in Hospital Settings Changing?" In E. O'Neil and J. Coffman (eds.), *Strategies for the Future of Nursing.* San Francisco: Jossey-Bass, 1998.

Kanter, R. M. "World-Class Leaders: The Power of Partnering." In F. Hesselbein, M. Goldsmith, and R. Beckhard (eds.), *The Leader of the Future: New Visions, Strategies, and Practices for the Next Era.* San Francisco: Jossey-Bass, 1996.

Kohles, M. K., Baker, W. G., and Donaho, B. A. *Transformational Leadership: Renewing Fundamental Values and Achieving New Relationships in Health Care.* Chicago: American Hospital Association, 1995.

Moses, E. B. *The Registered Nurse Population, March 1996: Findings from the National Sample Survey of Registered Nurses.* Rockville, Md.: U.S. Department of Health and Human Services, Health Resources and Services Administration, Bureau of Health Professions, Division of Nursing, 1997.

Murphy, E. C. *Leadership IQ.* New York: Wiley, 1996.

O'Neil, E. "Nursing in the Next Century." In E. O'Neil and J. Coffman (eds.), *Strategies for the Future of Nursing.* San Francisco: Jossey-Bass, 1998.